D1477273

practising architecture

Stiff + Trevillion
practising architecture

Foreword

There are plenty of well-designed and presented books about contemporary British architects. We were not sure whether our work really warranted a book, we have avoided the cult of celebrity and our work reflects that. Too many profiles offer a two-dimensional snapshot of the firm that is in reality a posh marketing brochure.

One of our young graduate architects was doing her Part Three exams, and I was her mentor. She asked how we had started the business and was astonished to hear that we were younger than her when we set up Stiff + Trevillion. She wanted to know more about it. This made me think that if we were to do a book it should be more than a parade of projects. It could be a story, not quite a modern fable in the tradition of Martin Amis' *Money*, but nevertheless a story of the highs and lows of being an architect. In a way *The Honeywood File* or *The Rubicon File* for the next generation. It would be great to think that this book is something that students might read and find helpful when doing their Part Three exams.

There is always good and bad luck involved in this business; it is a combination of chance and strategy. Perhaps most importantly it is about friends and mentors, without the likes of Doug Clelland, Peter Murray, David Rock, David Rosen, Simon Silver and Richard Cook our practice would not be here today.

Ultimately, it is a story about friendship and trust, between the founders, their colleagues and their clients, and always with the support of our long-suffering families.

Mike Stiff

PREVIOUS PAGES Portobello Dock. Overview of the Canal Building looking west with the iconic Ladbroke Grove gasometers in the background.

OPPOSITE Mike Stiff and Andy Trevillion on the roof of their High Street Kensington offices, 1988.

OVERLEAF Mayfly Cottage, view into main living space, showing double-height volume.

7

Contents

The key to success in any field is, to a large extent, a matter of practising a specific task for a total of around 10,000 hours.

Gladwell, Malcolm, *Outliers, the story of success*, London: Allen Lane, 2008.

Stiff + Trevillion is an architectural practice based in London. Quiet but never anonymous, the practice does not advertise, they do not need to. Their stream of commissions is maintained almost entirely by word-of-mouth recommendations. Few people will have heard of them outside the rarefied domain of the construction industry, they do not build 'icons'. Nor do they set out to express their own egos through their work, rather, their buildings allow the personality of the client to shine through.

From modest, often-insecure beginnings in 1981, Stiff + Trevillion now have a permanent staff of around 40 people, some of whom have been with them since the early days. They have a diverse and loyal client base, which includes international restaurant chains such as Jamie Oliver and Costa Coffee, blue chip developers such as Derwent London, and high-profile residential clients such as Adele and Damon Albarn. They have translated their talent and expertise into a business which has continued to thrive over the decades even throughout, probably, the most extreme global economic recession ever.

Less concerned than many designers with passing fashions in architecture, Stiff + Trevillion's work adheres to more traditional design principles, both of its time and positioned within a recognisable convention. It bridges the evolution of twentieth century modernism towards a highly articulate form of moulded spatiality. This ensures functional rigour in planning terms, combined with more timeless three-dimensional aesthetics: their interiors use modulated light to create dramatic yet intimate spaces, a technique more commonly seen in nineteenth century buildings like the Soane Museum. To this they add a controlled palette of materials, rich with diverse textures and flavours, providing spatial and sensory emphasis only when it is appropriate. They always consider the client's views as paramount, the most important element within this complex endeavour.

Although they started out as a duo, Michael Stiff and Andrew Trevillion were joined in 1989 by another partner Richard Blandy and, in 2004, by a fourth partner, Daniel Campbell. During the early years, whilst sometimes struggling to stay afloat financially, they gathered around them a coterie of reliable, long-term collaborators and accumulated a broad knowledge, slowly building towards their collective "10,000-hours" of expertise. For each of them the journey from apprentice to master craftsman has been arduous but rewarding. This is the story of that resolute journey.

Mark Dudek

Phoenix Brewery, sculptural
timber battened desk.

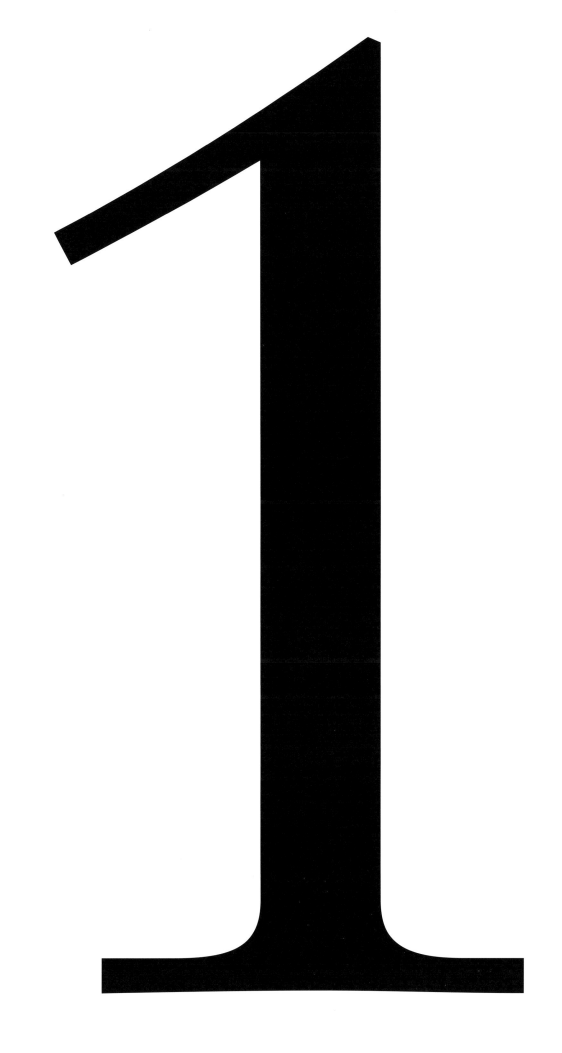

The 1970s

STUDENT DAYS

For Mike Stiff the choice of a career in architecture was an informed compromise. Although his father was also an architect, he entered the profession against his advice. He wanted to go to art school but was persuaded by careers advisors to work towards something more vocational, perhaps technical drawing. Unsure of his future direction he took art, history and sociology at A-level. On the strength of his portfolio he was accepted with alacrity at the Polytechnic of Central London (PCL), now the University of Westminster.

Fate seemed to be leading Stiff inexorably towards architecture and he realised that the subject reflected what had been his two main interests at school: firstly drawing and painting, a passion from his earliest years, and secondly an, as yet barely understood, interest in the social structures of the city, its exuberance and vitality, in contrast to the spatial ambivalence of his home in suburbia. This connection to buildings and space enabled him to combine two ideals: understanding and exploring the built environment, and expressing this sensitivity through drawing and painting.

Andrew Trevillion's choice of a career in architecture was linked directly to his interest in history, inspired by a particularly engaging teacher, together with his childhood obsession and undoubted skill in the construction of treehouses and self-build dens of every shape and form imaginable. He recollects being presented with a large T-square by a next-door neighbour on his sixteenth birthday, which probably sealed the deal.

PREVIOUS PAGE   Covent Garden 1975, queue outside the Royal Opera, when the market was still operating.

OPPOSITE   The Westway in the 1970s. Initially it divided the city, today however, the undercroft has become a well-used part of west London.

WHY STUDY ARCHITECTURE IN LONDON?

In 1974 Stiff, aged 18, headed for London and enrolled on the architecture degree course at PCL. The capital represented the promise of escape from a dreary home-counties existence, a place where everything was going to happen, where his life would really begin.

For many provincial kids like Mike Stiff who, from a distance, had watched the 1960s unfold in 'swinging' London, the UK's capital was suddenly the focal point for new ideas in art, music and design. Lured by the exciting climate of the avant-garde, even The Beatles had deserted Liverpool and moved to London for good by early 1964.

Although by the early 1970s the hey-day of British popular culture seemed to have waned, the capital's social life was still engaging and vibrant if you were young and curious; David Bowie, Roxy Music and the art school groups partly inspired by The Velvet Underground and Andy

Warhol were in their first youthful ascendancy; whilst in the latter part of the decade the new Punk movement exploded onto the music scene with a distinctly political tone, bringing some much needed anti-establishment energy and kicking open the doors for the 'art of opposition'. Suddenly the Sex Pistols were performing live at the Central School of Art, The Clash were playing at Dingwalls, Malcolm McLaren and Vivienne Westwood were opening their first punk fashion shop—Sex—on the King's Road, Chelsea.

For Londoner Andrew Trevillion, the choice of PCL was more prosaic, based on logistics (it was only a short walk from his home on St John's Wood High Street) and his love for his home city—where could be better than London to make his future career?

LONDON AND THE CLIMATE OF SOCIAL CHANGE

In the 1970s, like much of the rest of the country, London was run-down and in many parts squalid and dilapidated. There were still numerous bomb sites across the city which had lain derelict and undeveloped since the Second World War and now the city was being subjected to yet another menace every bit as disastrous as the Blitz itself—the municipal plans to drive an urban motorway—the city ring road—through many of the best parts of central London, including Knightsbridge and Maiden Lane. The old Covent Garden fruit market was closing down and the whole area was due for demolition to make way for the new road system. The first stage of the so-called "box" ring-road, Marylebone Flyover, had been completed and opened by Desmond Plummer in 1967, and by 1970 the elevated section of the A40, running up from Marylebone Road out towards the west was in place, effectively severing what had been a coherent north Notting Hill community.[1]

After years of neglect, the public realm was tatty and unloved. In the 1970s new architecture was largely commercial but unimaginative, shoddy and cynical, a watered down modernism verging on the brutal. You could count the decent modern and contemporary buildings on one hand, maybe two: Lasdun's early work (before the National Theatre), Hallfield School, the College of Physicians in Regent's Park; the Royal Festival Hall, largely designed by Leslie Martin, was good, as was Erno Goldfinger's Trellick Tower, the Finsbury Health Centre and Highpoint One by Lubetkin, the Smithson's Economist Building, and the Trades Union Congress in Bloomsbury. Not a very long list for a major European capital and player on the world stage.

The 1960s had been portrayed as an optimistic decade of change. Exciting scientific advances, particularly space exploration, resulting in the Apollo moon landings of 1969, played out across the nation via live TV, albeit in grainy black and white. A generation of children like Mike Stiff looked towards a bright, exciting future; a 'brave new world' no longer rooted in the past, where technology would improve the quality of life and provide endless possibilities.

19

This dynamic spirit of change somewhat regressed during the early part of the following decade, nevertheless the seeds of the Technological Revolution were still being sown. Pong, the irritating electronic tennis game, appeared in pubs up and down the city, the Sinclair pocket calculator arrived hinting at the digital possibilities to come (prior to that logarithmic tables and slide rules were the only way to do calculus). There were no word processors or online search engines. Today, it is almost impossible to conceive of a time before mobile phones and computers but in 1974, for a lot of people, the only way to communicate was in person or from a red public telephone box on the street. Only 50 per cent of UK households had a home telephone.

Since the early 1970s wider social opportunities had been emerging for young people, with access to higher education no longer confined to the privileged six per cent as in previous decades. Progressive left-wing governments had been promoting an egalitarian agenda since the mid-1950s and were now finally delivering results, providing mainstream educational opportunities for the many, instead of limiting them to the few. In effect, if you could get a few A-levels under your belt you could now access a university education along with the public school boys.

Local education authorities even provided a non-refundable living allowance for the duration of further education courses as an incentive to encourage less affluent families to send their children to the new red-brick universities, or their vocational equivalent, the polytechnics. At the height of the post-war welfare state the student grant was a meagre but almost survivable living allowance which did not need to be paid back at the start of graduates' working lives. In his first year at college Mike Stiff also benefited from a place in one of the highly subsidised halls of residence, in this case, a tower block on the PCL campus in the heart of Marylebone. Trevillion shared a flat in St John's Wood with his brother and friends.

For working class students, despite the lack of creature comforts, this was in many ways a golden time, ripe with possibilities and opportunities, which their parents had never even dreamed of. In the face of rising unemployment it was logical to take advantage of the offer to continue their studies rather than risk joining the ever-lengthening queues at the dole office. An entire generation were given the financial independence to leave their home towns and make contact with a wider world of new experiences and ideas. Having tasted such freedom, most of them would never return.

Like other areas of commercial life, architecture courses were attracting a whole new generation without the previous obligatory public school background. Many were grammar school boys with a handful of A-levels and an art school temperament, less interested in the business side of the profession and more tuned into changing trends in art and music. "Phony Beatle mania has bitten the dust", but Joe Strummer and The Clash (amongst others), were sending out a similar message regarding the authenticity of youth, or perhaps the idea that anything was better than what the 'old farts' were doing.

An oppositional culture, at times verging on the nihilistic, was infiltrating the professions of architecture and industrial design, formally the province of old men, infusing them with a new creative energy. Other soon to be allied professions were now emerging too, such as graphic design, advertising, fashion and furniture design, galvanised by this second generation of aspirational young men and women. The digital revolution was still ten years away, but an intuitive sense of the potential for new technology to transform the creative industries for the better was in the air. Things were ripe for experimentation in most avenues of the arts and also in the businesses allied to them; London was certainly calling.

LIFE AT THE POLY—MIKE FINDS HIS FEET

Stiff had enjoyed his first year and found his tutor Eldred Evans to be an inspiring teacher. In the second year, the PCL degree in architecture was broken down into a number of so-called "interest groups" or "units". Knowing little about the theoretical basis of each tutor's pitch, it was easy to get stuck in a place you didn't understand or even agree with, through a combination of limited choice and sheer ignorance. This happened to Mike Stiff when he joined Frank Harmon's Modernist unit in September 1975.

Unbeknown to him it was to be a pivotal year in the development of an alternative view of architecture. Opinion would soon move on from the rigid, dogmatic exclusivity of 1950s high modernism towards postmodernism and a renewed interest in the historical city. Harmon was American, an unreconstructed Corbusian modernist and something of an ideologue, who saw the Modern Movement as the answer to all of society's ills. Design strategies were based on a limited number of typological precedents, usually high-rise, high-density housing blocks in roughcast concrete. These were described in pseudo poetic imagery, like "streets in the sky". Lots of maritime references were employed to liven things up, such as "deck access", "gang-plank" walkways and "porthole windows", all reminiscent of a transatlantic cruise liner.

In reality much of the output of the Modern Movement as far as London was concerned, proved to be appalling. For Harmon's students there were study trips to gruesome housing estates in south-east London such as the now demolished Ferrier Estate in Greenwich.[2] Like the uncompromising chorus from *Animal Farm*, "four legs good, two legs bad", the Modern Movement screeched its own mantra, "rigour, truth to materials and honesty". For Mike Stiff it felt like a secular form of puritanism.

There appeared to be one set solution to the complex question of new social housing provision in London, there was little scope for any debate. Like a TV quiz, if you did not trot out the required answer, you risked

almost certain failure and a quick unceremonious exit from the game. For his major second year project, Mike was made to design a new housing development adjacent to one of London's most treasured public spaces, Primrose Hill, based on the Unité d'Habitation, an 18-storey mega-block in Marseille, designed by Le Corbusier in 1952. For Mike, no amount of enforced intellectual engagement could make this approach feel right.

Perilously ignoring the rules, Stiff conceived a scheme almost entirely without consultation with his tutors, proposing terraces of three-storey houses around shared gardens, similar in scale and texture to the surrounding Victorian housing. He had heard about Oscar Newman's concept of "defensible space", however beyond that there was little or no precedent or solid architectural theory to support his thesis.[3] Stiff found the unit's ideology to be out of touch, he was more interested in what was appropriate for London, and how the project would affect those who would use it—did it feel right? This meant a concern for those everyday details that people would see and feel, and a respect for the scale and context within which new buildings were introduced. He believes that this instinctive sense of appropriacy has directed the work of his practice ever since.

Although his sketchy explanation was enough to secure a grade just above fail, by the end of his second year Stiff was feeling dispirited and confused. He found himself gazing wistfully at the Saint Martin's School of Art summer show, seriously considering leaving architecture and opting instead for a career in fine art.

However, fate intervened once more and a discreet approach at the Primrose Hill final review helped convince him to carry on along his chosen path. A young charismatic tutor with a soft Glaswegian accent and an appearance to match, declared that despite the widespread censure he liked Mike's project and invited Stiff to join his third year interest group. His name was Doug Clelland. Starved of any previous encouragement, Stiff was elated and duly signed up.

LIFE AT THE POLY—ANDY FACES A DILEMMA

For Andrew Trevillion, growing up in St John's Wood was an exciting time. It was a predominantly wealthy, louche and cosmopolitan area of the city, full of interesting people and places. Like many of London's inner suburbs, the area still has discernible boundaries and a distinctive soul, with pockets of working class council estates sitting next to the mansions of the very wealthy. A century before, the area had attracted comparable artistic luminaries such as Lawrence Alma-Tadema (1836–1912) who was well acquainted with the then fashionable Pre-Raphaelites, and sculptor Fred Onslow Ford (1852–1923). Now, with the world famous Abbey Road recording studios and Lord's Cricket Ground, the area was attracting famous residents such as Paul McCartney, Mick Jagger and David Bailey.

ABOVE Professor Doug Clelland.

OPPOSITE The Rosetti public house, St John's Wood. A rare example of a modernist pub, sadly now demolished.

Before attending PCL, Trevillion spent his spare time in central London, typically visiting the National Gallery and the British Museum, with the occasional sortie to Squires in Carnaby Street for his shirts and shoes or a night out at The Lyceum. St John's Wood contained numerous pubs, clubs and music venues, which attracted outsiders to the socially diverse neighbourhood that Trevillion called "home". Quirky modern buildings such as the St John's Wood synagogue, and the Rosetti public house, jostled with the white Georgian terraces of Little Venice and the huge villas along Avenue Road bestriding the northern boundaries of Regent's Park. Much of Trevillion's interest in architecture developed through his knowledge of the histories of buildings, often-ritualistic follies, in, or close to, St John's Wood. For Andy it was all about people and the stories they had to tell.

Some of the figures within his orbit there were budding intellectuals such as PCL architecture student Bill Greensmith, but most were ordinary working class blokes like himself, keen to make their mark in the world. For example, Stuart Goddard, soon to morph into new romantic pop singer Adam Ant, was a friend. More importantly, Andy's milieu was peopled by so-called "faces", some of them chancers living in the grey area on the edge of the law; tradesmen and taxi drivers he met in the pub, bouncers and fishmongers, C-list theatricals and musicians, all of them somehow connected to men higher up in the ecosystem, the movers and shakers who were to prove crucial to the later development of Stiff + Trevillion's practice. In the pre-digital age, networking was based more on chance encounters in pubs and bars or through old school friends. You needed an outgoing personality, a thick skin and lots of charm to fish in this river. If you were willing and able to put yourself about, it was a convoluted but effective way to extend your influence. In fact, a few years later, one such chance encounter in a pub helped to secure the first significant Stiff + Trevillion project.

Enrolling at PCL in 1973, Trevillion had taken various part-time jobs with friends and faces from St John's Wood to make ends meet. One in particular was for Nigel Wright, an ex-gold smuggler and a friend of his uncle, who had set-up a retail clothes business called Dicky Dirts (as in 'shirts'), which was doing extremely well. Between his first and second year, Andy had taken nine months out from college to travel in the United States, after which he spent a few months working for Nigel. In 1975 he resumed second year at PCL having lost touch with his contemporaries and knowing none of the other students. The group around Dicky Dirts on the other hand, of which he had become an integral part, seemed like much more fun and was helping him to earn good money. He asked himself if, in this time of deep economic recession, it was really the right moment to be embarking on seven years of arduous unpaid study. Shouldn't he be launching himself instead into a lucrative business with his mentor Nigel Wright? Did he really want to become an architect after all?

23

At that time the newly-installed head of PCL was Allen Cunningham, who had introduced a somewhat liberal attitude to architectural theory, quietly diluting the ideological drive of the Modern Movement die-hards, preferring to triangulate between modernism (without the socialist ideology), the decorative arts in general, and Neoclassicism, along the way gathering together a much more eclectic team of unit leaders than the previous regime. These diverse figures brought to PCL a sense of intellectual curiosity and a new dynamism. They were, it seemed, in constant creative tension, which frequently culminated in arguments and full-blown slanging matches, often played out in public.

The design unit themes ranged from the scholastic classicism of Demetri Porphyrios, who inspired Prince Charles' stylistic revival of all things Palladian, through the former Archigram member David Greene (co-founded with Cook, Herron, Crompton and Webb), purveyors of a late form of quirky utopian modernism originally inspired by Theo Crosby. During the same period, the 'inside-out' engineering style called "high-tech" was gaining ground as the natural successor to Brutalism, with two influential new buildings being hailed as ground-breaking—the Pompidou Centre in Paris by Piano and Rogers, 1971–1977, and Norman Foster's Sainsbury Centre which opened in 1978. This approach was promoted by unit leaders such as Don Genasci and New Zealander Andris Berzins, but, to Mike and Andy's tutor Doug Clelland, it was of little relevance, a stylistic development of modernism's limited and moribund agenda, a case of 'the Emperor's new clothes'.

When Doug Clelland teamed up with Mexican architectural historian Alberto Perez-Gomez, and subsequently for the diploma with a youthful Eric Parry, to form a new unit—the "urbanists" or "anti-rationalists" as they were sometimes called—sparks flew. As a group they occupied the opposite extreme to the Modern Movement rationalists led by Peter Jenkins and his acolyte, Andrew Peckham. Clelland, Perez-Gomez, Parry and a number of others were informed by a much longer time frame than the limited post-Enlightenment science and technology boys. Inspired by Architectural Association guru Dalibor Vesely, they were developing new philosophies, which established the role of Hermeneutics and Phenomenology as part of an alternative architectural discourse.[4]

Among the degree students this new unit was initially viewed with scepticism, an attitude that probably stemmed from the impenetrable intellectual terminology that characterised it, and many found dizzyingly incomprehensible. Having only just been given creative licence to explore conventional topics, the last thing these students needed was to be confused by ideas in opposition to the conventional art and history agendas. However, a small number of students found their ideas compelling. Modern Movement theory (as opposed to modernism) seemed to be past its time and they were inexorably drawn to the need for a new approach, anything was up for exploration.

24

The prevailing belief within the urbanist group was that everyone else in the department had got it wrong except for Clelland and his cohort. For previously disaffected students like Mike and Andy, it was a potent and engaging mix. On joining the Urban unit, they felt they had finally found their tribe, and in Clelland a leader worth following.

Many schools of architecture during the 1970s had dismissed history as largely irrelevant. There was little coherent sense of graduated historical narratives with new developments in architecture reflecting subtle and evolving shifts in social values. Rather, history tended to be used as a formalistic support mechanism for Modern Movement ideologies. Inevitably this meant over simplification, starting at the Renaissance and Palladio, then straight into the Modern Movement via Violet Le Duc and Louis Sullivan. The problem for the urbanists was not that they weren't interested in the great Modernist pioneers or their individual buildings, in fact these were a great source of inspiration. The problem was the application of rationalist principles on an urban level as these were out of scale, ignoring as they did the social and spatial complexities of the historical city. They wanted to be modern yes, but not at any cost.

JOHN BRANDON-JONES

To counter-balance his eclectic choices in appointments of unit heads for design, Allen Cunningham's approach to staffing the history course at PCL was more conservative. While many of the unit leaders were budding intellectuals, fired by new thinking and full of creative energy, few had real life experience of building. These teachers were encouraged to talk about the past in a personal way, bringing history to life through their own direct experiences of the buildings and people who had influenced them. This made strong retrospective connections for the students back to the pre-Modern Movement pioneers such as Charles Rennie Mackintosh, William Morris and John Soane.

A good example was John Brandon-Jones' history course focussing on the Arts and Crafts Movement. He had joined the partnership of Charles Cowles Voysey (son of Charles Voysey) in 1933, where he had designed a number of provincial town halls in load-bearing stone, with centralised hierarchical plans. These were buildings with a simple gravitas, which spoke about the weight and stability of local government supporting communities. His work was grounded in the classical tradition, though stripped of most decorative elements, and respectful of its context, sympathetic in feel to the RIBA building in Great Portland Street. Nevertheless his buildings were considered regressive, at odds with the progressive technological ideology of the Modern Movement, with its free plan and lightweight curtain walling.

At the start of the Second World War, as a naval officer, Brandon-Jones had been posted to Scapa Flow in the Orkney Islands, and put in charge of the engineer's drawing office. During this time he encountered three rare houses designed by William Lethaby, which he helped to restore.

Thereafter, he became a much-respected authority on Arts and Crafts domestic architecture, publishing widely and continuing his architectural career specialising in the refurbishment of pre-war houses in that tradition. He refused to accept that the Modern Movement was the only approach possible in the twentieth century, indeed he argued that high-rise modernism, widely viewed as a viable solution to the post-war housing crisis, was complete folly. His controversial opinions eventually began to affect his academic career. Previously, Brandon-Jones had taught at the Architectural Association but because it was feared that teaching the students about the Arts and Crafts might undermine their confidence in the Modern Movement, in 1969 it was politely suggested by the then Head of School that he should leave.[5]

Some might say that in 1973 he was an Arts and Crafts relic in his own right: he came to lectures wearing a pin-stripe suit and bowler hat, always carrying an antiquated snuff box from which he took regular pinches, which he inhaled deeply as he addressed the students. Trevillion felt a deep, personal connection to Brandon-Jones, he had an almost mystical allure, like some wise but eccentric, ancient bard, telling stories from his time capsule of accrued knowledge. Such was the lack of interest in Brandon-Jones' particular take on architectural history that he often lectured to only three or four students at a time. On one memorable occasion Trevillion was actually the only person in the class. Unfazed, Brandon-Jones delivered his class eye-to-eye with Andy as if this was the most normal thing in the world. Trevillion viewed this as an exceptional privilege and coolness personified.

While for many of his contemporaries, history of this kind seemed irrelevant to their view of architecture, to Trevillion it was like discovering the keys to a treasure chest. It was these history lectures more than anything, which kept Trevillion engaged during the first two years of his studies, and convinced him that a career in architecture could really be fulfilling. It was in a Brandon-Jones lecture that he first met Mike Stiff and discovered their shared fascination. From that moment on, their friendship developed and the two men's paths began to intertwine. The lure of Dicky Dirts and the promise of all that easy, filthy lucre faded into oblivion as his focus sharpened.

DOUG CLELLAND, DEGREE AND DIPLOMA—MIKE LEARNS TO DRAW

Much of the innovation in big business appears to be a happy accident, born out of luck rather than planning. Corporate innovators make their own luck—they force connections, try things out and never give up. This is 'the science of serendipity' and to benefit takes determination, provocation, experimentation and political savvy.[6]

Following a depressing second year, for Mike and Andy third year with Clelland and Perez-Gomez was an epiphany. It quite literally saved Michael Stiff's architectural career, such was the galvanising effect the new teaching team had on him and some of the others in the group.

Clelland and Perez-Gomez, each in their own style, were deeply committed teachers, immersed in the history and culture of architecture, in art, philosophy and politics generally. They were dissatisfied with the limitations of modernism—architecture for them was never just about building. Their strength as a team was that they moderated each other's extremes. Whilst Clelland could be crushingly rude and very volatile when students did not work with the commitment he expected, Perez-Gomez was cooler, detached, a more sensitive foil for the Glaswegian's directness. Conversely, when he felt sometimes that his assistant was too conservative in his advice, Clelland encouraged their students in fearless experimentation. Imagination was the essential, liberating ingredient.

Lectures were illustrated with slides of places they had previously only dreamed of visiting. While for students today low-cost flights mean it's not particularly unusual to fly off and visit Prague, Barcelona, Rome or Lisbon, back then it all seemed very exotic and glamorous. The holistic view promoted by their teachers that culture, history and buildings all come together to make a place, resonated with the group. They discovered the notion of appropriateness of materials and forms, and sought meaning in design rather than simplistic functionalist solutions. Norberg-Schulz and Wittkower were the key texts that enabled them to understand this concept of the city.[7] They discovered the Baroque and other branches of Classicism, such as Mannerism. They began to explore Georgian London with Summerson and Cruickshank and began to intuit why almost forgotten figures, like Soane and Mackintosh, were so important.[8] They learned about the Surrealists and the Situationists, Umberto Eco, Jackson Pollock, the Cubists, Louis Kahn and the New York Five. An art school approach to the conceptual representation of architectural ideas was encouraged. In the pre-digital age this meant all sorts of interesting mediums such as collage and photo-montage could be explored: the means of representation were critical and had to go beyond the usual Rotring pen-and-ink drawings scratched onto sheets of tracing paper.

These tutors understood that their students learnt most about the uniquely three-dimensional art of architecture by actually visiting buildings and cities, not just gazing at pictures in books. True understanding of their historical context was an act of critical observation and the best way to tune into this was by sitting before them, immersed in the context, and drawing them. They communicated exactly what it meant to design buildings with a cultural sensitivity and productive openness, rather than with a reductive, closed-off mentality. Clelland and Perez-Gomez both viewed architecture as a vocation, and most importantly, sincerely believed that it had to be informed by a narrative.

"Do you know this-or-that building or book or film", was the constant refrain during tutorials, which were almost always one-to-one. Cultural references were broad. The tutors challenged students to go away and seek out new knowledge themselves, to broaden their minds and their horizons and learn how to apply abstract information to their developing understanding of architecture. Sometimes, after studio, they would all

KANCELÁŘSKÉ POTŘEBY   DÁRKY   ŠKOLNÍ POTŘEBY

go back to Clelland's flat at Marble Arch to drink whisky and talk about architecture into the small hours. The enthusiastic students found their views suddenly listened to—they were treated equally. To Mike and Andy it felt like being at an Oxbridge College: thrilling, fertile, compelling, un-dogmatic—everything their previous year had not been.

A key strategy of the third year programme was to dispatch students to see as many relevant buildings at first hand as possible. Modern masterpieces were certainly included such as Le Corbusier's Villa Savoye, Adolf Loos' Villa Müller in Prague and the Maison de Verre in Paris, by Pierre Chareau. They also discovered more off-beat references worth exploring: quirky follies such as the Rushton Triangular Lodge in Northamptonshire, a complex Trinitarian symbol building from the seventeenth century, with no discernible function whatsoever, except for

its secretive embodied rhetoric was one of the many compelling examples of the new approach.

Design strategies in studio abandoned the straightjacket of the earlier year's programme (a functionalist approach which generally meant room schedules were developed into building forms), and were based instead on narrative or metaphor so that they could be read on a number of different levels—this was all about interpretation and meaning.

One of the earliest visits Stiff + Trevillion made together to study a building in situ was to the Soane Museum in Lincoln's Inn Fields. The sheer density and spatial complexity they found there was a revelation—was it a house or a museum, this palimpsest of plundered memory? The large family house Soane started to build in the 1790s was completed 40 years later. They were curious that the two ideas appeared to sit side-by-side quite comfortably; that you could actually design one thing, which could develop as it evolved into something else. In terms of domestic architecture, this functional flexibility was a particularly important lesson for them. Within all the clutter, the strength and structural clarity of the architecture shone through, maintaining a crucial sense of order. That subtle balance between pure clean lines and the ephemera and accrued references of everyday existence that people collect throughout their lives, was to become a key theme in much of Stiff + Trevillion's later design work, particularly in relation to residential commissions.

Back in college both historical and Modern Movements in art and architecture were now up for reappraisal and plunder in design studio discussions. For example, the very roots of Classical and Gothic architecture were exhumed for ironic reuse, some would say misuse. Any reference to 'aesthetics' was banned. Stiff's final degree project was proof of this fertile climate—a collage of dreams at Vauxhall Cross. It was a fantastic ruin with apartment blocks in the form of gigantic Corinthian and Ionic columns both upright and fallen randomly across the site. At

OPPOSITE Drawing of a graphics shop in Prague, Mike Stiff, 1993.

ABOVE Maison de Verre, Paris, Pierre Chareau, 1928.

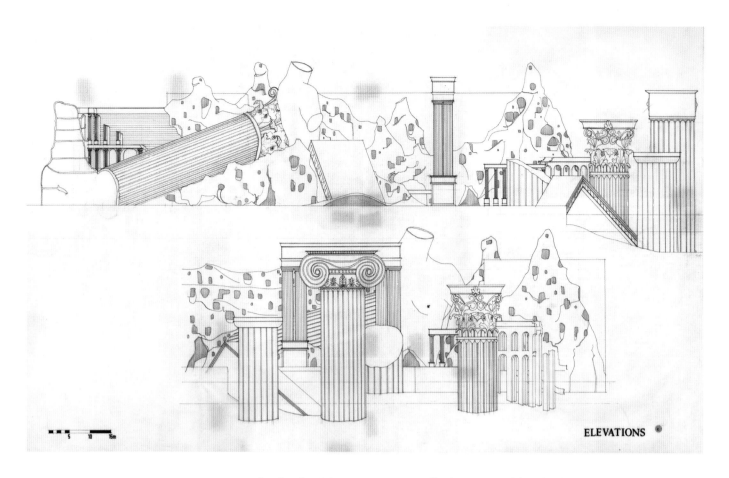

ELEVATIONS

the final critique it was soundly hammered by the head of history, Alan Colquhoun, who viewed it as wilful and lacking in academic rigour. Stiff, he pointed out, had failed to differentiate in gender between the 'female' Ionic order and the 'male' Doric.

But it didn't matter, the project was richly imaginative, a theme park Forum Romanum, with narrow streets and alleyways, traditional urban squares and campanile towers from Baroque Rome and Renaissance Florence, all composed with the gleeful *joie de vivre* of the young and uninhibited, a collage of styles and forms from history, happy in its playful ignorance. It was witty, iconic and precisely drawn, creating a stir when initially revealed at the examination and later during the public exhibition. Like a number of the other projects on view, it was a provocation, a punch to the solar plexus of the rigorously po-faced 'rationalists' presaging Charles Jencks' publication, *Post Modernism*.[9] Their external examiner, James Stirling, loved it and came up with his own curious 'collage city' when, a few months later, he designed the Wissenschaftszentrum in Berlin (completed 1988). The story goes that he came into his studio with a pocket book on architectural styles, directing his assistants to organise undigested historical forms around a central courtyard. There was to be a basilica, a cruciform church, an amphitheatre, joined-up to an existing Classical building and all selected randomly. "We'll have one of each", he is reported to have decreed.[10]

After the success of the third year with Clelland and following their year-out in practical training, a strong clique of like-minded students, led by

ABOVE Dreams of Vauxhall Cross, Mike Stiff Diploma scheme, 1977.

OPPOSITE The Soane Museum, section through the mausoleum, Mike Stiff, 1988.

Mike Stiff, returned to PCL for their diploma, treading water until the sixth year when they would rejoin the maverick Scotsman. This time his partner was Eric Parry.

Eric spent much of his time sketching vigorously in his moleskin notebook, notching-up all manner of idiosyncratic details and observations like an artistic magpie, mixing architectural and literary ideas in numerous rapid sketches, all the while stroking his wild, Byronic hair. Eric was a restless spirit, never satisfied, always seeking out new ideas, a footloose cosmopolitan *littérateur*. In those days his personal life was somewhat chaotic and he notoriously lived a semi-nomadic lifestyle living on a double-decker bus parked in the Roundhouse car park in Camden. Every so often he would disappear off on some mad road trip. When one day three post-graduate students turned up for their Tuesday morning tutorial they found the bus had gone, along with Eric, and they returned to Marylebone Road wondering whether, had they arrived a few hours earlier, they would now be on their way up to the Hebrides with their unpredictable tutor. Later Parry took-up residence in Clelland's office in the School of Architecture, lying low until the janitors had switched off the lights and locked the doors, content to use the drawing studio by night to progress his projects into the early hours.

The influence of Parry's drawings and sketchbooks was felt by the whole unit, Stiff in particular. The primacy of his drawings was new to the Modern Movement period of architectural studies, connecting the hand to the brain in a way that Maria Montessori would have approved, when she stated that "the hand is an extension of the brain".[11] Indeed in some ways the basic premise of that year's teaching was for the students to become childlike again in their take on the world, to dream and to foster spontaneity and to become ever more imaginative. For Clelland, these young people were a group of talented young artists in his care and he had a duty to defend and protect their creative freedom like the Praetorian Guard, no mean feat in those reactionary times. In return, each student had to find their own way to carry the torch and communicate this spirit and their own singular truth through their work.

For Stiff it was sheer bliss. He started painting again, initially making representations, not only of the things he saw whilst analysing the site, but also of his own architectural designs, mostly in mellow watercolour washes. However, over time he found there was a lack of precision about this technique, not enough 'exactness', which was requisite for the discipline of architecture; it was too 'art school'. The realisation made him start his search for an alternative medium.

The Soane Museum had illustrated the important connectivity between plan and section, showing at first hand that in urban architecture controlling this relationship was particularly important in the modulation of natural light and in developing spatial complexity so that it was more like a city plan, full of layered mystery. The question was how did you combine two almost contradictory representations in a single flat image?

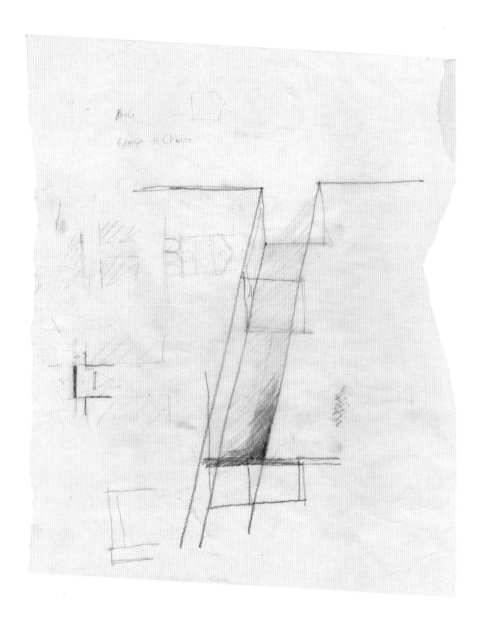

Firstly, the measured precision required of an architectural drawing (important since the contractor took his dimensions off when it was being constructed); secondly, the passion and emotional spirit required to turn building into architecture, prose into poetry.

He had observed Parry using pencils and coloured crayons freely in his sketchbooks and was impressed by the sense of movement they gave and their capacity to communicate light and shade, and provide subtle emotional nuances. Crayons and a sketchbook were also easy to transport and use in the field, more so than watercolours. He realised that he could combine a measured elevation, section or plan, drawn lightly in pencil on textured cartridge paper, using some of Parry's rendering techniques. With Derwent coloured pencils sharpened to a fine point he could mix subtly different tones using rapid directional lines and accurately control the outline, then give the image an overall texture which emphasised the interior form over and above the external shape. This type of drawing technique had been partly demonstrated when Parry ran some studio workshops, however, Stiff took the technique, honed it and returned to studio a week later with a completely new intimate evocation of light and space on a flat measured set of architectural drawings, which combined the required precision with more emotive qualities, giving the drawing its life and humanity.

It was a form of craftsmanship, which, after college, evolved further, culminating in numerous presentational images not just of his own work but of buildings and settings of a highly architectural quality. They possess the cool, quiet beauty of a landscape or a still life painting together with the ordered accuracy of traditional architectural rendering. Over the next ten years Stiff would make numerous trips on his own to interesting locations abroad—Cuba, Portugal and southern Italy—with his camera, sketchbook and crayons, giving free reign to his joy in drawing.

Drawing had become an important act of creative renewal but also a marketing tool, which communicated the finer aesthetic judgement of the main designer of Stiff + Trevillion's practice. Stiff's early drawings—now highly collectable—became an important adjunct to the design work in the practice during the early years. Stiff remarks that often clients would discover the drawings at exhibitions or in a journal, become intrigued, and later commission the practice on that basis, rather than on a portfolio of built work (as at that time for the practice, built projects were still negligible).

THE ROME PROJECT—COMPLETING THE DIPLOMA

During the late 1970s, there was a concern about where city planning was going, how its new architecture was balancing the needs of the modern world with the values of the historical city—the big issue was context.

In London and New York this had come to wider public scrutiny when the demolition of two iconic nineteenth century monuments—the Euston Railway Arch, 1961, and Penn Railway Station, 1963—went ahead despite widespread public opposition. The indifference with which these acts of destruction were permitted seemed to many like wanton vandalism, an attack on the architectural heritage of these two great cities, and this worried the establishment.

Even today, 50 years later, for many people sitting on a double-decker bus as it dawdles past Euston Station, the two remaining rustic stone pavilions framing the empty plinth where the monumental arch once stood is a melancholy sight. Inscribed with northern destinations such as Crewe, Blackpool, Carlisle and Glasgow, the once symbolic gateway to the north is now pathetic rather than romantic, its absence resonating down through the intervening decades.

The demolition of these iconic buildings posed the question of how and why we protect old buildings in the context of a voracious new form of capitalism which seemed to value individual developer's profit over shared cultural heritage—urban renewal was all about the bottom line.

A feeling was also growing in London that the soul of the city, its real life relevance to public and private lives, activities and events, was being squeezed out to be replaced by a much more closed and private focus. As an act of solidarity, Mike and Andy and some of their acquaintances demonstrated outside the old Billingsgate Fish Market on its last trading day in May 1979. Subsequently the vacant carcass of Billingsgate was closed forever, converted into another city dealing house, a commission undertaken by that great defender of London's public spaces, Richard Rogers. Commercial expediency at its most cynical?

Against this backdrop the diploma students were beginning to make sense of the historical precedents which were unfolding in lectures, seminars and tutorials. In April 1977, *The Fall of Public Man* by Richard Sennett was published. It spoke about the failure of modern architectural theory to promote spaces, which were functionally and socially mixed, therefore

The Euston Railway Arch
being demolished, 1962.

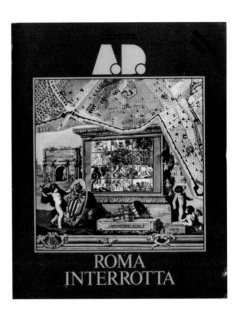

ROMA
INTERROTTA

'urban' in a traditional sense. This was followed soon after by Colin Rowe's *Collage City*, 1978, a celebration of Rome and its richly textured layers of history, creating compelling, yet chance, collisions of style, texture and time.[12] Critically informed opinion was now addressing the issues, which were concerning the society around them, and what they were learning seemed suddenly current and relevant; new ways of looking at architecture were fascinating and sexy and they mattered.

In this context, Rome was being gradually rediscovered as the main theatre of ideas, not just about the preservation of urban culture but also in relation to the question of how the public realm should be reinvigorated. Whereas in Britain, Thatcher was extolling the virtues of 'car culture', in Rome and Paris people could still view the city with all its public and private spaces appreciatively, the traditional city with streets, squares and alleyways, tightly enclosed by semi-public built form mediated by people walking. These were spaces through which you promenaded for show, or in which you simply hung-out, sitting in a cafe with a cup of coffee enjoying the view and people watching. For a relatively short period of time this idea was once again at the forefront of architectural consideration and widely recognised as a more suitable template for the design and conservation of cities.[13]

Around this time the influential periodical *Architectural Design* published a double issue "Roma Interrotta".[14] Guest edited by Michael Graves, it invited a number of celebrity architects to suggest design interventions in "The Eternal City". However, the learned articles about Mannerist Rome along with the influential Giambattista Nolli *Plan of Rome*, 1748, contributed more than the plans for 'interruptions'—design ideas on the existing city. With its subsidiary public spaces such as churches and theatres hollowed-out and shown as contiguous with the clearly defined public streets and squares, the beautifully executed Nolli plan showed the city as it was intended to be. In his concluding article, Alan Chimacoff stated "[These projects] suggest that cities are resistant to a singular view no matter how poetic, humanistic or sensible that view might be, and that, generally, effective alterations must be small-scale, incremental, contextually responsive, culturally related, and probably slow in materialising and maturing."[15]

Clelland decided that the fifth year project would be set in Rome, or more precisely it would be located on sites within the ancient city's most sacred and iconic area, the ruins of the Forum Romanum. A field study trip was organised as the lynchpin of the year, which entailed intensive city walks in the mornings, followed by afternoon sketching sessions in and around the Forum. Everyone would then meet up for drinks and dinner in the evenings, a social dimension which complemented the academic focus of the daytime activity and was central to Clelland's idea of *civitas*. Despite the fact that they were really tourists, the students were encouraged to play at being active participants of the public realm in Rome. At one point each student was given a plastic bag and asked to spend a couple of hours rooting around for historical

OPPOSITE *Architectural Design,*
"Roma Interrotta" issue,
vol 49, 1979.

ABOVE Hill House, the west
elevation, Mike Stiff, 1983.

fragments in the Forum, each like some sort of latter day Lord Elgin. The unspoken aim was that these fragments would be handed over to later decorate Parry and Clelland's new commission, a solid-state electronics factory in Oxfordshire.

Douglas Clelland had been a bright, sports-obsessed Glasgow schoolboy with little interest in architecture. He played cricket for Scotland and was on the edge of international selection for the Scottish rugby team. However, around the age of 16 he discovered Hill House on the outskirts of Glasgow and became fascinated by the client Walter Blackie and those who had lived there. With its sophisticated plumbing and invisible geometric order, the residence seemed to effortlessly combine the utilitarian with something altogether more spiritual: a melding of architecture and nature. Clelland subsequently directed his intellectual curiosity into all things architectural.

In 1971, having qualified as an architect with a first class degree, Clelland became determined to go and work for one of his heroes—the famed Philadelphian Louis Kahn, who, combining modernity with deep historicism, had designed buildings including the stunning Kimbell Art Museum in Texas, 1966–1972, and the monumental government buildings, Sher-e-Bangla Nagar in Dhaka, Bangladesh, 1962–1983. Having received no reply to several letters, Clelland flew out to Philadelphia, waiting on the great man's doorstep for several days until Kahn finally appeared. After talking to the young Glaswegian for an hour Kahn gave him a job on the spot. Clelland then spent several years as an apprentice before returning

ABOVE Kimbell Art Museum, Texas, Louis Kahn, constructed 1969–1972.

OPPOSITE TOP Cill detail, Collegio Romano.

OPPOSITE BOTTOM Students with tutor brawling in the streets of Rome, Mike Stiff, 1980.

to the UK to take up a teaching post at the Architectural Association. He had learned a great deal under Kahn, and much of this valuable knowledge would eventually be communicated to his students, almost as a form of legend.

Clelland was a romantic soul who fully subscribed to the idea of the rich complexities of the historical city—its layering of events and the drama of human experience and the opportunities it afforded for liaisons and interactions of every kind. He was a curious and erudite man whose idea of a perfect evening was to trade literary references with the likes of Dalibor Vesely, David Leatherbarrow, Daniel Libeskind and Joseph Rykwert at the Architectural Association bar in London—competitive debates aimed at showing who knew most. Clelland assembled knowledge about everything which could inform his architectural discourses—important quotations written into notebooks with meticulously pasted illustrations of places, people and objects. Here was the scholar at work, seeking chance encounters and ideas that might provoke those moments of serendipity when creativity and inspiration are sparked into life.

The evenings in Rome took on a typical routine for the group: intense discussions and arguments in local bars and restaurants, fuelled by the local wine, albeit with the students often floundering in the intellectual chasm between them and their erudite teachers. Little small talk was permitted when Doug held forth. Although middle class to the core, he would often revert to the working class Glaswegian humour he had learnt at school, sometimes crude but always charming and insightful, a sort of architect's Billy Connolly. The anecdotes were tempered with immense intellectual curiosity and insights into art, architecture and culture in general, a combination that made him great company. He loved to see his students losing their inhibitions, becoming outspoken and raucous and expressing exactly what they felt.

Following these dinners, drinking sessions would extend into the night, which then usually fragmented into smaller parties of partially inebriated students roaming the streets on the look-out for edgy bars and nightclubs. Occasionally there was a fracas—a street brawl with locals, or the loss of something or someone from the party. The tale of Trevillion's wallet which, having been lost in St Peter's Square on the first evening miraculously reappeared intact, held aloft by a Dominican monk at the airport departure gate on their return, became legend.

There were guided walks every hungover morning, energetically led by the two tutors, Clelland usually leading from the front. From time to time the more relaxed Parry would hang back to pick up some of the stragglers such as Chris Balme and Andy Trevillion. Detached from the main group, Andy would make fascinating and slightly subversive side visits, for example, to study the highly mannered cill rustication on the Collegio Romano, a feature which would appear 25 years

KEY
A. ENTRANCE to APPARTMENT
B. COURTYARD
C. RETAIL
D. WORKSHOP
E. BAR - RESTAURANT
F. SEMI - PUBLIC ROOM
G. HOSTEL
H. CURIA
I. S.LORENZO
J. BASILICA ÆMELIA

PLAN 0 5 10 15 20

ROMAN FORUM   MICHAEL STIFF

ABOVE Diploma Forum Project,
Mike Stiff, 1980.

OPPOSITE Plan of the Palazzo
Massimo alle Colonne, Rome,
Baldassarre Peruzzi, 1532–1536.

later on Parry's facade for the renovated Lancaster Hotel in West London. The students feasted on the sumptuous Baroque churches of Borromini, observed his competitor Bernini's mocking riposte at the Fountain of the Four Rivers in Piazza Navona and visited Keats' House overlooking Piazza de Spagna. All of these buildings and the intoxicating atmosphere of Rome itself, heavy in the air like the stupefying incense of its churches, galvanised the group to take the maddening challenges of the Forum project head on. It was a full-immersion in every sense.

One of their most influential visits was to Palazzo Massimo alle Colonne, a masterpiece of mannerist city architecture halfway along Corso Vittorio Emanuelle II. Although closed to the public, Parry and Trevillion managed to sneak past the porter through its beguiling facade to explore the colonnades and courtyards, which lay behind. Designed by Baldassare Peruzzi in 1532, it is overtly contextual, yet adopts a surprisingly modernist architectural language in both facade and plan. With its urban setting and the linking of spaces in complex asymmetrical series (much like Soane's Museum) it felt reassuringly complex. Unlike the high rennaissance *palazzi* of Palladio, which tended towards an autonomous form of rustic simplicity, lacking in contextual intelligence like up-tight wedding cakes, Palazzo Massimo quite simply looked amazing and felt 'right'.

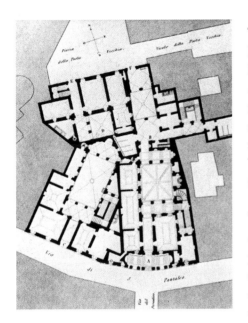

The form comprises of what appears to be a centralised entrance loggia beneath a subtly curved external skin, which contrasts with the flat linearity of the adjacent buildings, echoing the slight change in direction of the street alongside. The effect of the curve in plan is reinforced by the facade's surface treatment. The rustication is not normal; rather it is sharp and linear, seemingly extruded uniformly over the entire surface of the building, giving it the appearance of a taut skin pulled across a frame. This elastic sensuality is further accentuated by the lack of definition at the edges.

The ground floor is seemingly set apart from the upper floors by an eccentrically enlarged projecting entablature from which the columns and pilasters appear to be hung. The entablature and indeed the entire facade are characterised by a duality, with the articulation of window and wall elements, expressing solids and voids, verticals and horizontals in a strange dissonant rhythm.

In plan the building is equally mannered. The seemingly conventionally balanced facade when related to the plan is not symmetrical at all. The entrance vestibule connected to an existing loggia at the back, was impossible to align axially. A narrow dark corridor leads from the central bay of the entrance loggia along the left side of a new cortile (rather than joining it at its centre). One is drawn into this space by the light coming from the older cortile beyond, (which had been retained from the original palazzo). However, one's attention is immediately shifted to a new axis of symmetry at right angles to the entrance, centring on a fountain at the side of the first cortile, which naturally aligns with the second cortile. These two dominant interior spaces are not axially aligned; rather they exist independently, aligned incrementally with the idea of procession based on an altogether more interesting and varied urban ordering. Rather than being rationally composed in a self-contained Vitruvian manner, this new ordering is contextual, in complex relationship with both the classical and the urban condition.

The dissonances, which exist between the part and the whole, are consistent with the ambiguities seen in the surface articulation of the facade. It is a form of Mannerism, which respects and understands the Vitruvian principles of balance and order, but deliberately sets-out to ameliorate and to some degree make them fit-in with the existing context. Through sheer creative invention, this building helped to define a new, more modern architectural language, which was complex and culturally resonant, seemingly relevant to the issues that faced architects in the new, postmodern world of the late 1970s.

This detailed but by no means comprehensive explanation of the building is important in the development of Stiff + Trevillion's later design process—Palazzo Massimo was a real discovery for them both. In particular the complicated relationship between plan and elevation, mixing the unbalanced with the balanced, an amusing trick which they

41

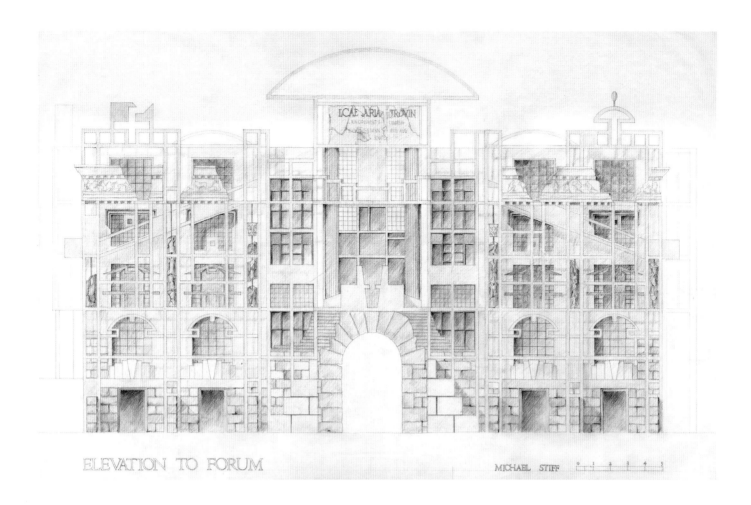

ELEVATION TO FORUM   MICHAEL STIFF

ABOVE Elevation to Mike Stiff's Forum
Project—apartment block on the Basilica
Aemilia, 1980.

OPPOSITE Luigi Moretti, Casa Il
Girasole, Rome, 1950. Perhaps the first
postmodern building.

both felt was a crucially important understanding, a eureka moment, one of the key-stones of their ongoing architectural cognition.

Although both Mike and Andy, are cautious about being overly analytical, it is clear that the Rome trip gave them important insights into the ways in which modern architecture could and should refer to both historical and modernist precedents without resorting to pastiche. It provided intellectual credibility during the first five to ten years of their time together in practice, giving clients confidence that these boys knew what they were talking about. However, for Trevillion, the Massimo experience added something else of equal significance to his increasingly eclectic interests.

Andy had attended a high-brow lecture course taken by Joseph Rykwert as part of third year history and philosophy course.[16] Rykwert was a fellow traveller with Vesely and very interested in the almost forgotten pre-Enlightenment philosophies of the Hermetic Tradition in Renaissance art and architecture. Trevillion was fascinated by the conflicted personalities involved in the movement and in the comparison of its precepts to the 'new' proposals of seventeenth century scientific movements at that time. He found his way into this by way of two key publications, which he devoured, *Giordano Bruno and the Hermetic Tradition*, and *The Art of Memory*, both by Frances A Yates.[17] He was becoming somewhat obsessed by the concept of architectural mnemonics and the art of memory used as a type of sign system in spatial design. This new intelligence emphasised hermetic geometric proportions, the use of explicit symbols to choreograph space and specific types of political space described in classical architecture. He decided to take the daunting subject on as his dissertation and consequently organised a meeting with the elderly Yates at the Warburg Institute in 1978. For the Rome project he was encouraged to try and apply the knowledge he was soaking up but the subject proved elusive, almost impossible to get hold of. All was not lost however, as it did afford important pointers in design terms for the future.

This intimate knowledge of the complexities of Rome and the reading of it that Clelland and Parry encouraged them to see, planted the seeds for the way in which Stiff + Trevillion's design ethos would evolve. There would be no house style adopted for its own sake, such as engineered 'high-tech' or Neoclassicism, and although Rome was full of Classical buildings, some good, some mediocre, Stiff + Trevillion's buildings would have none of their forced symmetry, no pediments or Classical columns, Doric, Corinthian or Ionic, no trace of the type of literal classicism given expression in Robert Venturi's extension to the National Gallery in Trafalgar Square in 1991.[18] They also vowed that new technology would not be adopted for its own sake, it would be used only if it added to the building's performance in some way, if it was appropriate. Everything would start from two key conditions, the site and the client. They would respond to the contextual needs of a given setting and combine this with what the client needed, accurately providing an intelligent interpretation of their vision. Where a column

MARK DUDEK

MICHAEL STIFF

ANDY TREVILLION

77 · GLOUCESTER · ROAD
· LONDON · SW7 · 4SS ·
01 373 0343

was required it might be characterised to create spatial emphasis but it would always be interpreted in a modern idiom. Projects would be small-scale in the sense that they would, with a few exceptions, be contextually responsive to the surroundings but expressed in a clean, uncluttered architectural language. If historical references were included in any of their projects, they would be subtle and abstract. Above all they decided that their practice would be based in the bustling, energetic environment of the city that they both knew and loved—London.

Each project, large or small, seeks cultural resonances, not by being fashionable but by being appropriate. There is a search for joy in the ordinary. The architecture of Stiff + Trevillion does not shout, it does not compete, it coexists in harmony with its neighbours, it 'fits in' to its context. "Cities are made of buildings interspersed with moments of sublime architectural significance", states Stiff

think about Piazza Navona, Sant'Agnese works because the curvaceous vitality of its facade, which is alone at the centre of an ordinary terrace of what could be described as background buildings. Its expression is a statement about its place in the city. It is a standout building but you could argue that the background buildings are equally important. Rome taught us to appreciate this distinction.

This philosophy has been remarkably consistent even after 35 years in practice—these are the founding principles, which determine every strategic decision the two architects take.

45

The outcome of the Diploma year in Rome was a highly contentious set of projects, some of them rather too ambitious for their own good but all of them brave and imaginative, set within the context of the Forum. For many of the students in Clelland's group the challenge set had been too difficult, perhaps more appropriate for a post-Diploma thesis. It set Clelland up for a series of often frenzied encounters with the external examiners in defence of his students, and verbal skirmishes with a number of internal critics. But because it had been his idea and the group had all gone along with it unequivocally, he returned their trust with his unwavering and loyal support. For a few of the students, Stiff + Trevillion among them, the task was successful, a short but deeply formative immersion in the oppositional architecture of Rome.

Trevillion wisely explored the interface between the Tabularium (Rome's Medieval town hall) and the northern edge of the Forum, a manageable problem because it had well-defined boundaries. Stiff on the other hand, utterly confident in his growing knowledge, took the challenge head on. Adapting the remnants of the Basilica Aemilia, he created a deconstructed facade for an apartment block. This was presented in such a way that few could question its architectural legitimacy and the scheme was expressed in three enormous, hand-drawn renderings, which combined sensitivity with power and drama and ultimately won him the Diploma prize. Perhaps more significantly it also provoked much wider publicity for the young architect, with one drawing featuring on the front cover of

OPPOSITE Drawing by Mike Stiff of the Umayyad Mosque, Damascus. The building was, in turn, a Roman temple, Christian basilica, and today is the fourth holiest place in Islam.

ABOVE The first business card featuring Dudek, Stiff + Trevillion. The typeface was influenced by the album cover for Joy Division's *Closer*, also featuring plans of Roman antiquities.

Building Design magazine. The set of drawings was also given a starring role at the annual Royal Academy Summer Exhibition where they visually dominated the architecture room, their monumental scale matching the subject and the space.

ABOVE PCL Diploma students relax in the Forum Romanum, 1980.

OVERLEAF Sketch of a bar in Rome, Mike Stiff.

— Don't just 'do' architecture: write, paint, do anything which adds to the practice's reputation.

— Savour your education and establish your own personal belief system.

— Seven years training should provide a design ethos; stick to it, do not be tempted to follow fashion.

— Think for yourself, avoid fashion and dogma.

— Study and work in groups, shared experience is invaluable.

— Architecture is about the everyday as well as the monumental.

— Challenge the brief.

CHAPTER 1 NOTES

1. In 1974 the market traders moved out and the site fell into disrepair. Most of the area was earmarked for comprehensive redevelopment. A public outcry resulted in the listing of over 250 buildings. In 1975 the GLC began major restoration of the old Covent Garden market buildings. It re-opened in 1980 with specialist shops and stalls geared towards tourists.

2. The Ferrier Estate, in Kidbrook was held-up as a model for new low-cost housing, hence the group visit. Aside from its dubious spatial qualities, it became a by-word for urban decay, one of London's worst burglary black-spots and the setting for the gritty 1997 film, *Nil by Mouth*. Its vast centralised heating system harboured a labyrinth of tunnels, which became a massive rat-run.

3. Newman, Oscar, *Creating Defensible Space*, Darby, PA: Diane Publishing Co., 1966.

4. Dalibor Vesely (b 1934) studied engineering, architecture, art history and philosophy in Prague before coming to London via Paris and the 1968 student riots. Having studied with Hans-Georg Gadamer, he established the role of Hermeneutics and Phenomenology, initially at the Architectural Association, latterly at Cambridge.

5. According to architectural historian Alan Powers, the then Architectural Association head wrote to Brandon-Jones with his concerns regarding the potential for Arts and Crafts theories to undermine teaching of the Modern Movement. Brandon-Jones decided that as he did not really wish to teach, he would resign anyway. He then returned to become a partner in Voysey's office. Powers suggests that this shows the Architectural Association's insecurities regarding the Modern Movement.

6. John Kao, creator of Harvard Business School's Innovation Program and Chairman of the Global Advisory Council on Innovation to the World Economic Forum.

7. Norberg-Schulz, C, *Meaning in Western Architecture*, New York: Rizzoli, 1980; Wittkower, Rudolph, *Architectural Principles in the Age of Humanism*, London: Alec Tiranti, 1962.

8. Summerson, John, *Heavenly Mansions and other essays on Architecture*, London: Cresset Press, 1949; Cruickshank, Dan and Peter Wyld, *London, the art of Georgian Building*, London: Architectural Press, 1975.

9. Jencks, Charles, *The Language of Post-Modern Architecture*, New York: Rizzoli, 1981.

10. Girouard, Mark, *Big Jim: the life and work of James Stirling*, London: Pimlico, 1981, p. 224.

11. Kramer, R, *Maria Montessori—A Biography*, London: Hamish Hamilton, 1978, pp. 286–287.

12. Sennett, Richard, *The Fall of Public Man*, Cambridge: Cambridge University Press, 1977; Rowe, Colin, and Fred Koetter, *Collage City*, London: MIT Press, 1978.

13. "Intelligent City" in *Prospect*, February 2013.

14. *Architectural Review*, vol 49, no 3–4, 1979.

15. Chimacoff, Alan, "Mannerism in Baroque Rome", pp. 28–35.

16. Rykwert, Joseph, *On Adam's House in Paradise: the idea of the primitive hut in architectural history*, London: MIT Press, 1981.

17. Yates, Francis A, *Giordano Bruno and the Hermetic Tradition*, London: Routledge, 1964; Yates, Francis, *The Art of Memory*, London: Pimlico, 1966.

18. Venturi, Robert, *Complexity and Contradiction in Architecture*, New York: Museum of Modern Art, Papers in Architecture, 1966.

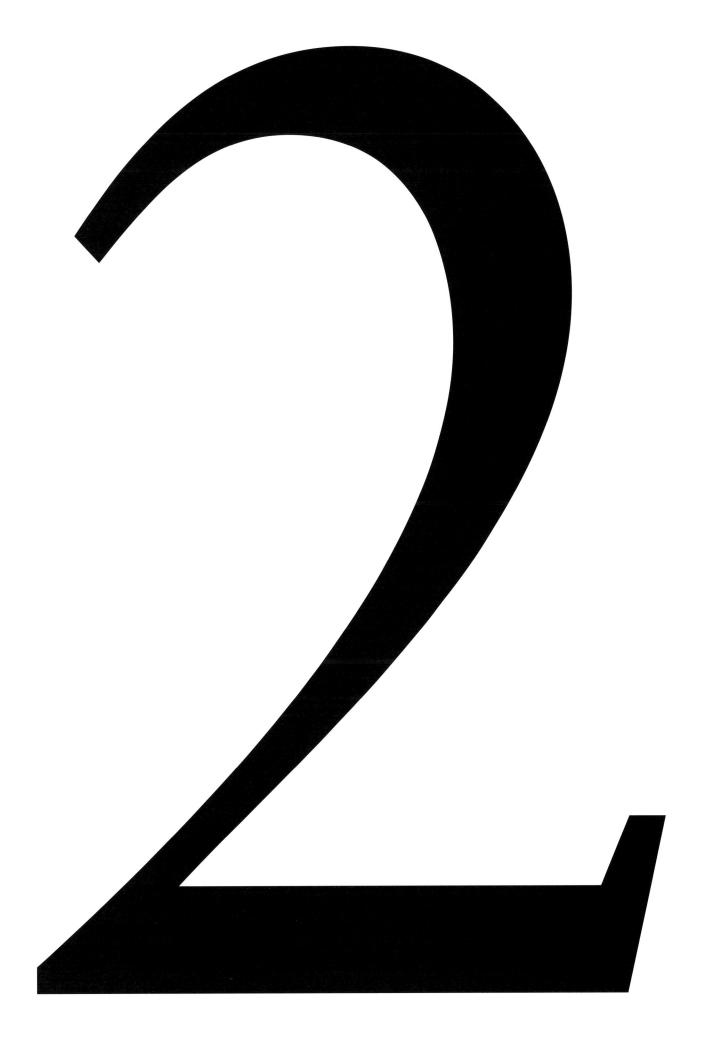

The 1980s

SETTING UP IN PRACTICE

A friend needs her house extending. She has a vague idea about what she wants but finds it difficult to envisage. She knows you're working for a large commercial practice in town and asks you to take the job on. In the meantime, you pick up another larger commission from a friend of the family. Suddenly you have the means to set up on your own. But why do it?

High-end architecture is a tough, vocational discipline, which requires a solid foundation based not only on creativity and design theory but also on extensive, practical experience and a degree of business acumen. Many young architects only eventually manage to master this complex humanistic art after many years of experimentation, certainly making a plethora of mistakes along the way. Having completed seven years of full-time further education, including a couple of years working in commercial offices but with little real responsibility, how fit are you to actually set-up in practice? How much do you really know about the business of architecture?

Most often the answer to this question is, probably not a lot. Having enjoyed studying for their degrees and having raced through their professional practice examinations without anywhere near enough on-site experience (a familiar catch-22 for many young architects), both Mike Stiff and Andy Trevillion were able to use the prestigious RIBA letters after their names by the time they were 25 and 27 years of age

PREVIOUS PAGE Richards Medical Center, Philadelphia, USA, 1957–1961, designed by Louis Kahn, an important source of early inspiration.

OPPOSITE Schuhmacher Meisster, East Berlin—a modest, pre-Second World War shop facade, pencil and crayon rendering by Mike Stiff.

respectively. However this, along with Mike's growing artistic reputation, was enough at the time to encourage various informal requests from friends and acquaintances for their architectural advice. Luckily some of these enquiries turned into real commissions.

Between degree and diploma, Doug Clelland had recommended Mike to a friend, David Rock. Rock Townsend was then a 15-person practice operating from a shared space at 5 Dryden Street, Covent Garden. David Rock and John Townsend had a liberal attitude to the business. Mike recalls that in that distant, pre-email era, the post was delivered to the practice twice a day, opened and then left on the front desk for all to see, information on salaries and pay rises was shared. The principle at Rock Townsend was that nothing was secret: if you made a mistake, you admitted it and accepted the consequences. Collaboration and trust in human relations was viewed as the key to good practice.

As a business, Rock Townsend was a rather radical departure from the traditional idea of how an architect's office should be run. It was a very social environment, transparent in its dealings with employees and clients and apparently lacking in unnecessary bureaucracy. It was part of a managed workspace concept, an idea pioneered by the architect-owners themselves, the first UK business to develop this into a working prototype. At its height the Dryden Street space was home to 65 firms, each able to achieve a degree of independence within this flexible and cost-effective accommodation.

Having seen how his own father's architectural office functioned, for Mike it was a revelation. The workspaces were laid out in an open-plan arrangement with various small firms sharing the same floor but separated by screens creating a degree of privacy. This gave the office an informal and democratic feel, everyone worked in the same space, no one could hide away. Decisions were made in the spirit of openness that was fostered by the space itself. There was a coffee station rather than an old fashioned 'tea lady' with a trolley, bicycles littered the entrance areas, there was even an art gallery. Architects, engineers, artists and craftsmen all worked together in Dryden Street, absorbed in their separate tasks but performing them side-by-side. If ever there was a form of architectural practice that positively affected behaviour, this was it.

For Stiff this period formed an important bridge between his sketchy, student knowledge of how an architectural business worked in practice, and real, self-sustaining, practical know-how. The happy year spent at Rock Townsend demonstrated to him that architecture could be both fun and ethical and a great many of the lessons learned from his year out, and from this and further stints at Dryden Street, helped formulate the template for the way his own practice would be organised in the future. The Rock Townsend model absolutely defined the way Stiff + Trevillion would work for the first 15 years, and to some extent today: the organisation would always have to be small enough to function on a single level with partners, architects,

ABOVE Rock Townsend's space at 5 Dryden Street.

OPPOSITE Pen and ink drawing of 5 Dryden Street, David Rock.

model makers and administrative support staff all essentially sharing the same creative environment, working side-by-side. Even today the office holds onto most of these principles with the emphasis on direct, effective communication.

Although he made some good contacts at Rock Townsend, Mike's post-diploma experience was less fulfilling. He went on to work for Chapman Taylor, a large commercial outfit in Kensington, where he was mainly occupied with drawing-up window schedules and reflected ceiling plans for huge provincial shopping centres in the postmodern style. Where Rock Townsend was seemingly devoid of hierarchy, at Chapman Taylor partners and directors were distant figures dressed in pinstripe suits that seemed largely oblivious to the existence of the younger members of the practice. Partners rarely fraternised with the "juniors", as they were referred to, and even had their own 'executive' floor where they worked in rarified isolation. Instructions filtered

The Place dance studio, King's Cross. Rock Townsend with Mark Foley. This was the project Mike worked on during his year out, 1977–1978.

down to Stiff and the other junior jobbing architects via Project Architects within the design teams, who were first briefed themselves by Associates and Directors, and often became garbled and imprecise along the way, like Chinese whispers.

At this time Nigel Woolner was a young partner at Chapman Taylor struggling to re-shape the business along Rock Townsend lines. The practice was changing but very slowly, like some giant archaic ocean-liner turning slowly mid-ocean. For Mike, working there was a largely dispiriting experience and apart from completing his final RIBA Part Three qualifications, the key thing he concluded from his time at Chapman Taylor was that if he ever had his own practice it would be structured in a very different way to this company—decisions about important design matters would always be discussed directly with all team members to ensure that everyone was on board and clearly understood their role. He recalled an anecdote he had heard about Leslie Martin, the great architect of the Royal Festival Hall, who rarely, if ever, convened a meeting.[1] Instead he preferred to walk around the office and talk directly to each person there, treating everyone from the office boy to the design guru equally and communicating with all of them directly himself. It was an informal but egalitarian and effective approach, and one which Stiff very much admired. Having experienced two very different ways of working at Rock Townsend and then Chapman Taylor he had now made up his mind and was determined that his own practice would be collaborative.

It was now 1980, one year before the two young architects would formally establish Stiff + Trevillion. While they worked through the dull projects they were given in the commercial practices they were apprenticed to, earning little and feeling under-valued, both began to work on small private projects in their spare time, building the odd house extension or two, working during the evenings and weekends and sometimes taking extended lunch breaks to visit their own projects on-site. As casual commissions arrived, the notion of setting up on their own began to seem deceptively easy and their youthful enthusiasm convinced them that starting a practice together should be the next step in their careers. Fortunately the wise words of warning that had been drummed into them by their Professional Practice tutor at PCL, Granville Pyne, still rang in their ears. The liability implicit in building was potentially limitless and setting up a practice was all about timing and having enough profit in hand to support their salaries. Jumping the gun and doing everything too soon was risky—they needed to hold fire and choose their moment carefully.

At this point Stiff + Trevillion still knew very little about business management but what their education had equipped them with was a strong, well-founded, self-belief as decision-makers within the sphere of design. They both had a lot of confidence in their ability and a certain amount of *chutzpah*. They were social and, each in their own way, charismatic. Both recognised the burgeoning need to network effectively in order to cultivate connections to the kinds of people who might, in the fullness of time, give them important commissions. Both knew that they couldn't build the sort of practice they wanted on home extensions alone—they wanted to move into the 'big time'. Architecture was to be their life and ultimately the commercial world of office developments was their goal, it would be most profitable and rewarding from a design perspective.

Whilst they did not set out with a coherent series of goals or particular objectives, there was a clear, if unstated, ambition between the two: the idea of building a robust, medium-sized practice, designing harmonious buildings in the spirit of Rome, referencing the art of memory and never losing sight of the client's views. These were aims, which were at once socially aware, innovative for their time and ultimately popular and profitable. Both men in their own particular spheres were starting to make connections which were bringing in tempting promises of work; Andy was developing interesting connections via the north London scene (over a couple of beers in St John's Wood he was introduced to John Murphy, the founder of the massive contractors of the same name) while Mike was connecting with influential cultural figures through his drawings, eventually leading to work on crit panels at PCL where he assumed the mantle of part-time tutor in his own right. However, although they were focused on the task of getting work, little thought

went into what would happen when it finally took-off and they had to start building and managing the business effectively. Despite their design credentials they barely knew what a fee forecast was, neither fully comprehended the crucial importance of cash-flow ensuring that fees came in on time in order to cover the monthly outgoings and they had few systems in place to properly manage the risks involved with running a business. The art of architecture was still their primary concern while their knowledge of the science of building was scanty. The construction of a coherent business plan for their new venture was, they felt, slightly beneath them—someone else could deal with that in time.

On 8 December 1980 John Lennon was murdered outside his home in the Dakota Building in New York. Lennon was one of Mike's all-time heroes and this event sparked into life an idea he had been toying with for some time but had previously shelved due to lack of funds: a research trip to the Big Apple.

Rome had been inspirational, however like most of Europe at that time, it was for the most part backward looking and antiquated. The architectural magazines of the day were full of exciting new late-modern and so-called postmodern buildings by the New York Five and other more commercial outfits.[2] He longed to check-out interesting modernist icons such as the United Nations Secretariat Building (which he had seen in the Hitchcock film, *North by North-West*), Frank Lloyd Wright's Guggenheim Museum and the famed Seagram Building by Mies van der Rohe and Philip Johnson. All of these legendary buildings he wanted,

in the words of Sherlock Holmes, to add to his "memory attic".[3] Not only did he wish to see them but to feel them, to experience them first hand, to understand their scale and context. Being somewhat obsessed by Picasso's work, in particular *Les Desmoiselles d'Avignon*, he was also keen to delve into the Museum of Modern Art's (MoMA) huge collection of modern paintings and, time permitting, he also hoped to visit Louis Kahn's Richards Medical Center (see p. 50), which Clelland had spoken so eloquently about. However, over and above all of this, what really attracted him to New York was the sheer awe-inspiring scale and intensity of its skyline, shimmering and glowing like a vertiginous coral reef, so different to any of the European cities he had seen. He wanted to understand that striking vertical impetus—how skyscrapers worked on the ground in purely urban terms, as well as soaring above the ground with such spectacular *bravura*. There was also something very dynamic about the American spirit of enterprise, so different to the somewhat staid way things seemed to be done in Britain, which inspired and galvanised the young architect to make the trip.

However, arranging a speculative trip to New York back in the early 1980s was far from easy. The type of cultural tourism that today is commonplace was difficult to justify in those days when money was tight and transatlantic flights were still prohibitively expensive, monopolised by the two flagship carriers, PanAm and BA, who naturally charged a premium. After the fifth year student trip to Rome, this was only the second time Mike had taken a flight of any sort and the romance of it would still excite him. Sitting in his cramped economy class seat, gazing out at the approaching New York skyline, he was entranced. This, he believed, was going to be a fundamentally important extension to his education and, hang the expense; ultimately it would be worth it.

Wandering through MoMA on his first day in the city he bumped into media-savvy London architect Peter Murray, complete with designer spectacles and foppish bow tie. It was pure serendipity and like Stanley and Livingstone on the shores of Lake Tanganika, the two English architects greeted each other with enthusiasm. They had coffee together, compared impressions, agreed to get together once they were back in London. English to his core, yet with an intuitive flair for the promotion of talented young architects both from home and abroad, Peter Murray was to become an important contact for Stiff in later years.

Murray was then the youthful editor of the *RIBA Journal*, later to set-up the influential *Blueprint* magazine and eventually his communications company Wordsearch. Even in 1980 when Murray was in his late 20s, he wielded significant influence and counted within his acquaintances the sort of high-end contacts within art and architecture circles, which Mike and Andy could only dream of. Mike's chance meeting with his compatriot on his first trip to New York illustrates that often luck favours the brave: that chance meeting in New York developed into an enduring friendship and led to critical recommendations, which later resulted in two pivotal commissions for Stiff + Trevillion.

Murray had studied at the prestigious Architectural Association during the 1960s and was the son of a local government official who was himself an amateur architect. In the evenings his father would draw up house plans for local builders. Although he was untrained and, according to his son, "the results would not have won any RIBA awards", nevertheless, a T-square and drawing board were part of the furniture in the Murray household when he was growing up. Another important influence in his youth was the developing Heritage movement. An interest in British history as seen through its buildings became part of the immediate post-war experience for many families. For the evolving middle classes it was more than just an excuse to get in the car and to go for a drive, it represented the search for an English identity after the upheavals of the Second World War. Beautiful buildings, particularly stately homes and their historical settings, were cherished, as they encouraged people to look back nostalgically to a rose-coloured, more innocent pre-war world, in stark contrast to the bomb sites and devastation which still scarred British cities. The popularity of this movement was eventually given formal expression through the first blockbuster TV series on the subjects of art, architecture and philosophy—Kenneth Clark's *Civilisation* in 1969.[4]

As a student Murray had been aware of the old-fashioned image the profession fostered, albeit unintentionally. While he believed that tradition had its place in the architectural lexicon, he also felt strongly that if the end result was not connecting with society then ultimately it had failed: architecture had to resonate with the general public either by thrilling them, comforting them or both. In the 1970s the tide was slowly beginning to turn—change was long overdue—and soon innovation would swirl through architectural design and practice on the crest of the punk wave that was about to sweep through popular culture. Murray relished the prospect of being in the vanguard.

He joined *Architectural Design* magazine when Monica Pidgeon was still editing it.[5] Murray persuaded her that a visit to Los Angeles was important for their readership since David Hockney, Ed Ruscha and Reyner Banham, amongst others, were working there, and their contemporaries from the Architectural Association—Alan Stanton and Mike Davies—were teaching at UCLA. On the back of his visit to LA, Murray wrote an entire issue of *Architectural Design* specifically on Los Angeles, a controversial decision at that moment in the history of this influential journal. Until then, *Architectural Design* had largely focused on the European city model and related forms of architectural expression—a city of a hundred suburbs and no centre had not previously been considered worthy of examination.[6] Now *Architectural Design* introduced new and influential figures to its British readership, such as Frank Gehry and Thom Maine of Morphosis.

Subsequently, Murray wrote a series of interviews for the construction industry weekly *Building Design*. He interviewed Frank Gehry, the first time an interview with the great man had appeared in a UK

journal, which led to regular commissions for the paper. A year later, he was offered the editorship. Like many high achievers, Murray had hardly chosen this career path, in a sense it just happened, growing spontaneously out of his own natural curiosity and charisma. He was soon poached from *Building Design* to become the editor of the *RIBA Journal* at the age of 35.

With the editorship of the profession's in-house bible in the bag, it seemed that he had arrived at the heart of the architectural establishment. However, rather than embedding himself there, Murray began to challenge the system, posing important questions about its future, questioning the image of architecture, and the self-important elitist relationship it had with the general public. During his days at *Building Design* in the 1970s, he had revealed the huge problems in prefabricated system building. He recalls watching a high-rise housing block under construction in Hounslow when a panel being lifted into position crumbled into pieces because the concrete had not cured properly.

He began to consider how antiquated techniques were in architecture, compared to other design industries such as fashion and advertising. Architects were increasingly viewed as an expensive luxury: it was a protected profession and as such it was under attack from the free-marketeers. Architects, believed Murray, had to raise their game and a good start would be transforming one of its most influential publications. The layout of the journal was duly designed to reflect a more contemporary feel, with new design features taking precedence over the somewhat hidebound concerns of the vested practice interests. Pension rights were all very well, but if the firms were to afford them, they had to become profitable, lean, able and willing to compete with the advertising and graphics boys.

In 1983 Murray started *Blueprint* magazine with a view to establishing a fresh voice about design and architecture featuring not just buildings but other elements, which help to shape the environment as well, such as furniture and graphics. Most importantly it would be a magazine that was accessible to a nonprofessional audience. He recruited Deyan Sudjic who was then writing for the *The Sunday Times*, someone whom he recognised could write about architecture in a way ordinary people could understand. Also, Simon Esterson had a similar connection in terms of layout and style, having designed *RIBA Transactions* for him a couple of years earlier.

Blueprint was intended to appeal to the younger end of the market and for the first time featured the designers themselves on the front cover (often with the buildings they had designed in the background). It set about turning architects from cryptic elitists with a faintly distant Masonic air, into more open personalities, ready and willing to communicate directly with the client base, and ultimately helped to create the first celebrity architects. In a similar way to the pioneering work of Nick Logan with *The Face* magazine during the early 1980s, *Blueprint* was youthful

61

ABOVE Elevation of the RIBA building in Great Portland Street, designed by Grey Wornam, drawn by Mike Stiff. This was commissioned for the *RIBA Transactions* magazine by Peter Murray following their meeting in New York.

OPPOSITE *Blueprint* magazine, December 1984, cover showing a youthful Richard Rogers with Mike Davies, John Young and Marco Goldschmeid.

and vainglorious. It regularly featured up-and-coming names such as Philippe Stark, John Pawson, Rick Mather and David Chipperfield across its eye-catching monthly front cover, driven by the desire to attract a wider audience through the bookstalls.[7]

However the idea behind the magazine also implied something more fundamental; it stated unequivocally that architecture was for people and that the new buildings, which were worth knowing about, would no longer stand in splendid isolation from those they were supposed to serve. Architecture was important but it was secondary to the real lives of people who inhabited the built environment. It was not an end in itself, it was the background against which their dramas, great and small, would be played-out, like the landscape in *Les Demoiselles d'Avignon*. To be a good architect, you needed to connect with your public, just as a writer, an artist, or even a chef needs to connect. In Murray's opinion:

I'm not sure it has been a good thing... architects and architecture have a higher profile now than at any time in my career, and a lot of very interesting and spectacular buildings are being delivered around the world. That's a good thing, but it impacts on an infinitesimal percentage of the world's population. The profession has thrown out its social agenda with the modernist bathwater, it has failed to provide any sort of service that effects the quality of the ordinary and it has lost decision making power in the process to contractors and project

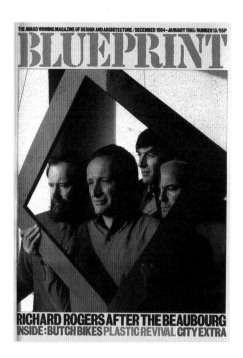

THE AWARD WINNING MAGAZINE OF DESIGN AND ARCHITECTURE / DECEMBER 1984–JANUARY 1985 / NUMBER 13 / 95P

BLUEPRINT

RICHARD ROGERS AFTER THE BEAUBOURG
INSIDE: BUTCH BIKES PLASTIC REVIVAL CITY EXTRA

managers. We have forgotten that architecture is a craft and architects are there to deliver a service that meets the twin demands of client and society, rather than satisfying their own vanity.[8]

In hindsight, it's clear that *Blueprint* never managed to penetrate the popular market in the way that, for example, Tyler Brûlé did some years later with *Wallpaper*, but Murray was one of the first to recognise that architecture could effectively be viewed as another form of branding and that this could be one of the new directions in which innovative practices could evolve. The commercial possibilities of the profession couldn't help but be enhanced by illustrating this coherently to potential clients, a point which was brought home vividly to Stiff + Trevillion when, as a result of the practice's revamp of the Costa Coffee shop chain, sales immediately rose in one central London outlet from 10,000 cups to 15,000 per week!

SETTING-UP IN PRACTICE AND BUILDING BIGGER

In spring 1981, Stiff + Trevillion finally took the decision to set-up practice together. Although their lack of technical know-how was a major concern, they reassured each other that what they didn't know about construction they would learn along the way. Things were gradually coming together for them and despite their youth, they simply felt that the time was right—Mike was 24 and Andy was 26.

Stiff + Trevillion was established on the basis that any money which came in would be split 50-50, after costs. The notion of equity was therefore established from the outset, equal profits, and equal risk for the two partners. In addition, they agreed not to undertake any public works, such as schools and hospitals, a decision, which was largely based on the limited architectural potential of such work and what they viewed as the overly bureaucratic system within which they would have to operate. Beyond that they were prepared to take on more or less any project, from the smallest bathroom extension to the largest corporate headquarters, the only limit was their own imaginations.

On a number of levels their timing was not fortuitous. Politically, the country was in the throws of sudden, cataclysmic change. The social stresses of a rampant trades union movement in direct and treasonous opposition to Margaret Thatcher's reforming government were very evident, and in certain industrial areas class warfare was rife. Industrial action in the form of national strikes had earned Britain the sobriquet of "the sick man of Europe" and on Fleet Street Rupert Murdoch was defenestrating the print unions with their antiquated lodges and heraldic rule books, as new print technology was making them redundant. The UK economy was on its knees. Dramatic and extreme monetarist reforms were being enforced in an effort to kick-start the economy. Inflation was running at an annualised level of 18 per cent and the plight was only worsened by Geoffrey Howe's 1981 budget, which increased taxes for most. "Ghost Town" was playing constantly on the radio, a leitmotif to the country's economic woes. The Brixton Riots lent dramatic witness to

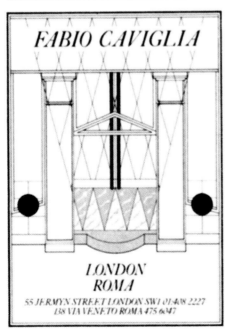

the young Left's oppositional zeal. There was a profound sense of change in the air—fear, anger but also optimism.

However, after two years in power, Thatcher's determination to revive in Britain a sense of self-reliance was slowly beginning to take effect and an entrepreneurial, can-do spirit was fostered, which actively encouraged new start-up businesses: the spirit of the age did not hold with the idea that only old men should be allowed to build.

Like many of his generation, as a school student Mike had been a socialist—a signed-up member of the International Socialists, selling the *Socialist Worker* on Newbury High Street on Saturdays and picketing Didcot power station. By 1980, whilst retaining his artistic and architectural iconoclasm, Thatcher's essentially working class pragmatism had caught his attention. He could see for the first time that one route out of the current economic crisis was to encourage people to stand on their own two feet and make their own success, if they could. Trevillion accepted Mike's somewhat reactionary philosophy but remained a committed socialist, (albeit one with champagne tendencies in his middle years), however they were ideologically tied to the humanistic architectural values which they had learnt about in Rome.

There was something dependent about the working relationship that had begun to develop between the two men, a close, trusting friendship as much to do with their shared world view, tastes and interests, as the business itself. Importantly they also shared a similar sense of humour, both seeing the ironies of life through a faintly cynical, world-weary lens. Both were dedicated and determined, functioning well on similarly punishing timetables, up and at it early every morning but also able to work all night if required. In terms of personality they were complementary. Andy was the laid-back Londoner who knew all the right places to go, a sociable man who enjoyed a drink and a chat, always cool and calm under fire, a personality full of humour, care and courtesy, a man who radiated granite integrity and deep kindness. Mike, on the other hand, was much more passionate and driven, somewhat hotheaded and inclined to be moody, at times outspoken and impatient.

The partnership has survived through thick and thin. Mike tends to do most of the high-end design, focussing on the big things, with Andy content to organise and direct in the background on the minutiae, giving Mike the space to do what he does and only sanctioning him when necessary. Mike on the other hand can galvanise Andy, fire him up, which he sometimes needs. Both are equally important roles in this symbiotic relationship, one would not work without the other.

By summer 1982, Stiff + Trevillion had successfully completed a couple of small projects together, a shop fit-out in Jermyn Street and a house in Norland Square for sinologist Endymion Wilkinson. They had also undertaken three or four international competitions, partnering Doug Clelland on an urban renewal scheme for Wilhelmstrasse in Berlin as

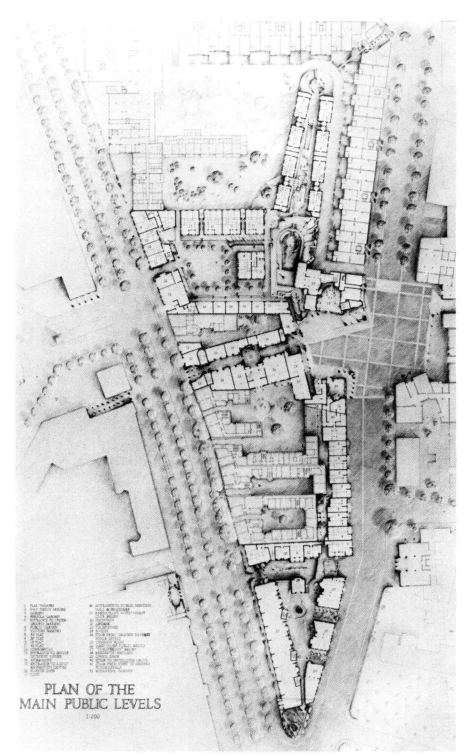

PLAN OF THE
MAIN PUBLIC LEVELS
1:200

13 Plan of the main public levels of Block 19

OPPOSITE TOP 37 Norland Square, London W11, fireplace surround for diplomat Endymion Wilkinson. This was their first large house commission, 1982.

OPPOSITE MIDDLE Fabio Caviglia, a former school friend of Andy's, commissioned this menswear shop in Jermyn Street, it was their first completed project as Stiff + Trevillion, 1981.

OPPOSITE BOTTOM Business card drawn and designed by Mike Stiff for the owner. During the 1980s many architects believed that the interior architecture and the graphics were inseparable—there was a tendency for some architects to try to design everything.

ABOVE Competition entry with Doug Clelland for a major urban quarter on Wilhelmstrasse, East Berlin, commissioned by the IBA (Internationale Bauausstellung Berlin) in 1984.

part of the ongoing building exhibition (IBA). Although their entry only came second in the competition, they enjoyed working on this large collaborative gig, interacting with some of the interesting brains involved. The experience left them wanting to build larger, as much to fill the now obvious holes in their knowledge as to scratch the itch, which had been started during seven years of thinking big at college. They felt they had spent the best part of a decade talking about architecture, now it was time for action.

WATERINGBURY, PRINCE CHARLES AND 40 UNDER 40

Trevillion knew John Gleeson, chauffeur to a Lebanese businessman, from his St John's Wood days. In 1983 Gleeson told him that his boss needed an architect for a small project in Kensington. Having recently flown from the chaos of civil war in Beirut, his chauffeur was a key confident, part of his circumscribed London network. Being less concerned about architectural reputation and looking instead for a good deal, in his eyes Stiff + Trevillion seemed young but keen, likeable and discreet. Above all they had an evident enthusiasm, a strong sense of purpose and were hungry for work. He believed that he would get his money's worth with their practice and that crucially he could keep control. From the outset the tone of the architect-client relationship was made clear, no *prima donna* tendencies would be permitted.

Initially Stiff + Trevillion were contracted to reconfigure the family's apartment. They enjoyed working with their new client who they found to be clear and decisive—he knew what he wanted and was not prone to changing his mind. There were no power struggles or last minute coded instructions after the latest trawl through *Homes and Gardens*. He was a businessman and, after the initial briefing, delegated the decisions to them as the experts. If they referred an extraneous matter to him he would tell them, "You're being paid to do the architecture, get on with it." It was exactly the sort of freedom that the young architects needed at that point in the evolution of the practice; it almost felt like being back in studio with Clelland. They revelled in his trust and the space he gave their creativity, and in return they performed well, were totally focused and committed to interpreting their client's vision. Once the overall shape of the project had been agreed, they were largely left to their own devices. The finished scheme was well received and the client was pleased with their work.

On the basis of that first successful commission, a year later the now thriving entrepreneur returned to the practice with another. Following the purchase of a large house in Kent, they were re-interviewed and, much to their delight, immediately appointed to extend and renovate the worn but beautiful Queen Anne residence. It was a three million pound project, which for them at the time was substantial. They sensed that this could be the turning point in the development of the practice and celebrated that night with friends and colleagues in their new after-work meeting place, The Britannia pub just off High Street Kensington.

Although this, their first significant project, was located in the country rather than in the city, a number of the Rome references still proved useful. It was a listed building, (Grade II*) predominantly in red Kent brick. There was a dominant main house with a lop-sided wing of outbuildings, old storerooms and stables. They were required to add a squash court, a gym, and a swimming pool with changing rooms.

The new building which housed these facilities sat in its own extensive landscape referencing the Greek idea that sport should be detached from

ABOVE High Street Kensington offices with pen and ink drawings of Portland Place lying on Mike's desk, 1988.

OPPOSITE TOP Wateringbury House, Kent, external elevation to the pool house bar, 1984.

OPPOSITE BOTTOM The original Queen Anne house was fully refurbished as part of the same commission.

other more cultural activities. It was also logical that this should be an adjunct to the existing nineteenth century utility wing. So a combination of brick and render was used, reminiscent of the Orangery at Kensington Palace. However, Trevillion treated this in a way that was appropriate to the twentieth century, with no extraneous decoration, relying instead on the landscape to provide texture, or what he referred to as "rustication", framing the new building in its semi-natural setting.

This early project sought to find meaning by tuning into its historical context rather than seeking a high-tech functional form, which might, in a different setting, have been more appropriate. Instead, a cerebral Louis Kahn-type response emerged. It featured adept, well-composed window-to-wall brickwork. It was refined, mature, stylistically conservative and, crucially, within budget. The project was an unreserved success and soon featured in all of the important design magazines, widely recognised as a surprisingly mature piece for such young architects.

The fees from Wateringbury enabled them to sub-lease an office space in west London. The decision to relocate to the west of the city was again

RIGHT 90 degree axonometric view of the Wateringbury development, colour pencil rendering by Mike Stiff, drawn for the 40 under 40 exhibition, 1988.

OPPOSITE Pool house showing the juxtaposition of brick and the rendered cornice.

the result of a chance encounter. Mike had met Nick Colwyn-Foulkes whilst working at Chapman Taylor. Nick had rented 1,000 square feet, near High Street Kensington and on running into Mike again suggested they share the space and resources, including a secretary. At last the practice had its first dedicated office address and it seemed to bring them luck: as well as the chosen location of their office, Kensington was where their Wateringbury client was located, the only big commission so far. They now had ambitions to become 'the' west London practice.

With a view to moving beyond the bread-and-butter residential work and up to the next level of project value, they entered into an agreement with Mike's architect father, John Stiff, and administered some of his projects. Working on industrial units along what had become known as the M4/M40 corridor, they concentrated for a time on building up a portfolio of larger built work, adding scale and what they felt was much needed credibility to their portfolio, with John Stiff as consultant. They then paid £30,000 to take a stake in John's small practice, borrowing from Barclays, who were obviously confident that the business was heading in the right direction. John Stiff was looking towards retirement and it seemed to make sense to merge the John Stiff Partnership with

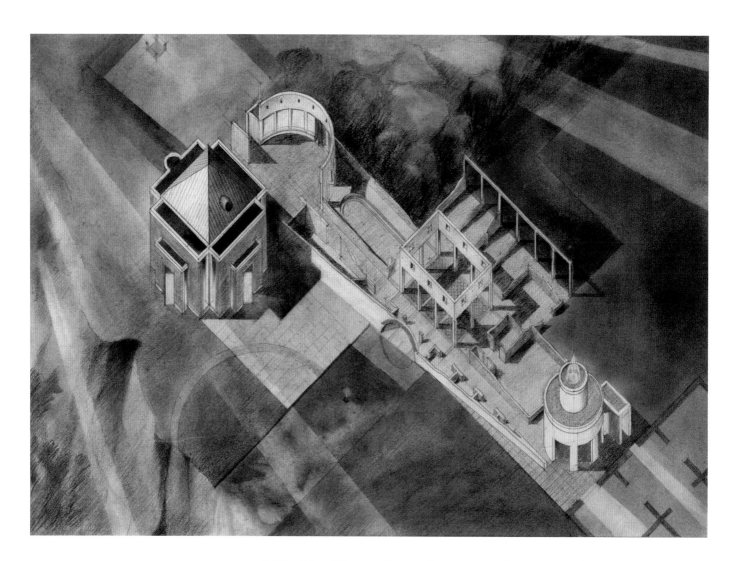

Competition entry for the extension to the Dulwich Picture Gallery, 1987. Note the arcadian landscape and water.

Stiff + Trevillion to form a larger complimentary whole. By now the business was beginning to epitomise the Thatcherite ideal—founded by innovative, youthful risk-takers it now had the support of an experienced practitioner to help them consolidate their business. Together they epitomised the next generation of commercial architects in the making. They were now confident enough to borrow big in order to grow and the banks were suddenly willing and compliant.

The chaos of the early-1980s faded with the defeat of the miners, and London's economy began to take off on the back of the North Sea oil bonanza. With Thatcher's success in the Falklands War, the decimation of trade union power was complete and when the controversial Conservative leader was re-elected for a second term, the green light was given for even more privatisation, which inevitably led to a re-inflated economy, and a mini-building boom and a plentiful supply of commissions for Stiff + Trevillion.

By the middle of the decade the traditional heavy industry bases of the West Midlands and the north were largely destroyed and the balance of power and wealth was now firmly focused on London and the south-east. London seemed to have detached itself from the rest of Britain and become part of Europe's wealthiest seam with a geographical profile which ran down to Paris, through central Germany and Switzerland, culminating in the Milan-Turin axis in wealthy northern Italy. This new powerhouse of free trade *sans frontières* was transforming the European economic landscape and was largely based on the service sector industries in which design was key.

For Stiff + Trevillion it had taken just five years to progress from being idealistic students sketching in the Forum, to business partners in what felt now like a thriving architectural practice. From the mid-1980s they were building offices and business park schemes for pension funds and private developers, mainly commissions which had been left over from the John Stiff Partnership. Although these projects were large-scale and profitable they lacked the cutting edge quality Stiff + Trevillion craved in design terms but on the other side of the coin, the private, mostly residential work they continued to take on was more a labour of love, engaging and intensive but ultimately not very profitable.

The partners now attempted to become developers in their own right. With an eye to the distant future they went, with John Stiff, to view a property in Tuscany: 39 arid acres with three run-down Medieval farmhouses loosely grouped together in a *borgo*. They travelled to Italy at the invitation of an artist they knew, Graham Bannister, who they had commissioned to paint murals at Wateringbury. Once there, they viewed the site, were charmed by the location and bought the property on a whim with the intention of converting it into holiday lets. In reality they had very little idea about the difficulties associated with such a venture, especially the Byzantine intricacies of Italian bureaucracy and property law. It was an act of instinctive, high-octane optimism based on the assumption that everything they did would go well, driven forward by their enthusiasm. Stiff + Trevillion were on a roll and celebrated the deal in a restaurant overlooking the Campo in Siena.

But the two were rather wilfully ignoring the things that were not going so well back in London and trouble was brewing. The Italian purchase was largely financed by another practice loan at a time when, except for Wateringbury—something of a happy accident—the steady flow of larger, more profitable, commissions that they had expected was not happening. They were becoming stretched financially and breaking into the architectural establishment was proving very difficult.

At this time the newly forming power brokers, people like Peter Murray, were painfully aware of the image architects and architecture had in the eyes of the general public. Architects were regarded with about as much respect as estate agents by most people and being a young architect in the UK often felt like being the least popular kid in the class. Attitudes within the profession were changing gradually and fresh new vision was emerging in some quarters, but the message was not really getting out beyond the incestuous confines of the RIBA. There was also a very political aspect to the architectural tribes, which were beginning to form in the 1980s. For a young practice like Stiff + Trevillion, knowing the

influential people to schmooze for each pitch and being in the appropriate camp was critical, but getting the choreography right was proving to be almost impossible. The vested interests, big commercial practices and their established network of client contacts and contractors, still very obviously ran the show.

Significant projects were still largely old school in style and conception, either Brutalist essays in exposed concrete of the Marcel Breuer lineage, or blockish office towers oblivious to their context in both materiality and form. For example, in his second year out at EPR, Trevillion had worked on a huge new office development, which utilised the air rights above Victoria Station. Its only 'innovative' feature was the use of then fashionable mirror glass, an affectation, which the project architects, had almost certainly seen on the Trump Tower in Manhattan. As he helped to develop this giant looking glass, Trevillion was exasperated: the use of materials seemed arbitrary, devoid of theory, faintly Disney-esque, all smoke and mirrors, with very little substance. He was concerned that to the outside world it may have looked like the usual two fingers up.

It seemed that the Old Boy's Network of the Establishment still had a tight grip on the UK construction industry but then in 1984 things took an unexpected turn when the spotlight of publicity was shone upon the profession during an event held at Hampton Court Palace, exposing it warts and all. HRH Prince Charles had been invited to address a room full of establishment architects celebrating the 150th anniversary of the RIBA's founding. The choice of speaker was surprising in itself since the

The property near Sovicille in Tuscany purchased by the business in 1987 as a long-term investment. It proved to be a rather short lived idea as it was sold on three years later.

Prince's views on modern architecture were well known. It is unclear whose idea it was to invite him to the celebration since he clearly held the RIBA in the lowest esteem, but a lack of political savvy at Portland Place had seemingly failed to assess the risk.

In retrospect, Prince Charles had that evening behaved like a softly spoken assassin in his black tie and fixed smile. His specific target was the winning design for the proposed extension to the National Gallery and as he rose to address the audience he took aim with both barrels of his gun, as if on a grouse shoot on the moors beyond Balmoral Castle. His speech was devastating, a carefully constructed critique of modern architecture *in toto*. It was indiscriminate in its savagery, reaching a memorable crescendo when he described the proposed new scheme as "a monstrous carbuncle on the face of a much-loved and elegant friend". Not only was it apposite but it also had a poetic ring to it, which appealed immediately to the right-wing media. Within hours, TV, radio and of course the *Daily Mail* were trumpeting his views to the nation, one lethal phrase splashed across headlines everywhere. That killer phrase and its shorthand, the word "carbuncle", has now entered the vernacular—in design circles there is little ambiguity about its meaning.[9]

The Prince's iconoclastic intervention had explosive repercussions, receiving extensive exposure right across the mainstream press. Significantly, his comments resonated with the views of the general public and could hardly have been more damaging or insulting to the old guard at the RIBA. For many people, it was a *schadenfreude* moment and a number of the prospective new guard, struggling young architects pushing back against the established conventions of their profession, secretly enjoyed it, perhaps considering the Prince's intervention to be timely, and for them, potentially advantageous. The RIBA elite tried to bite back, but failed to find much of a foothold: the views of Royalty in the UK are sacrosanct and carry tremendous weight, as long as they resonate with the populist views of their subjects. This view, expressed so waspishly, clearly did just that.

Ahrends, Burton and Koralek, authors of the first National Gallery Sainsbury Wing scheme, were considered to belong to the old guard. It was designed in the spirit of the Modern Movement, and to many critics already seemed old-fashioned and perhaps dysfunctional within its historical urban setting. Whilst there was some sympathy for them, they were respected professionals and decent people after all; they effectively became the scapegoats in this battle of architectural taste. The RIBA were convinced a radical response was needed to staunch the flow of bad publicity, PR would not be enough, but like a rabbit caught in the glare of oncoming headlights, they were stunned and nonplussed as to how they should react.

A series of exhibitions and talks on the Modern Movement and the merits of Brutalism were hastily organised. Lasdun's new home for the National Theatre had recently opened near the river and for a time was given star billing as the saviour of modernism. Then it seems the RIBA was infiltrated and things took a new turn. The recently appointed Events Coordinator was David Dunster, a politically astute operator with an enlightened view of the new architecture. His favourite architect, Robert Venturi (a big fan of Borromini's *S Carlo alle Quattro Fontana*) was commissioned along with partners John Rauch and Denise Scott-Brown to design an alternative version of ABK's winning scheme. The project was undertaken in the best academically precise Roman Mannerism with the use of a Classical order identical to the original, allowing it to blend easily into its historical setting. Not a progressive moment in the development of new urban architecture, but a project very much of its time—in the absence of a new approach, a reversion to the tried and tested.

The one positive thing that could be said to have resulted from the "carbuncle speech" was that it effectively acted as a catalyst for change, which sliced straight through the establishment and brought the views of a *Blueprint* generation into powerful focus. In the years that followed a broad consensus began to coalesce around the idea of the new architecture and what it should represent, focusing in particular on the idea of youth. Whilst the then RIBA President Rod Hackney was banging the drum for community architecture, he was also a non-dogmatic advocate for any architecture which was not LCC inspired 1950s modern. No one at the RIBA may have actually said it out loud but many were feeling that the only way to shake things up was to skip a generation, to start examining the ideas and work of a new wave of architects educated in the postmodern age. There were even suggestions that the RIBA building in Portland Place should be sold off, and a newer, funkier HQ building procured to give the profession a fresh face. In 1985, probably as a direct result of HRH's now infamous speech, the first British 40 under 40 exhibition was collated for the show at the RIBA before going on to travel around the country.

Whilst in most of the creative professions the idea of being under 40 hardly qualified as being young at all, in architecture historically it had always been the case. As if to emphasise the irony, the primary criticism that was levelled at this nakedly ageist show was that there were actually few completed works by the so-called next generation. Most panels comprised of drawings (and some models) of competition submissions and other unbuilt projects. Although admittedly there had been a recession in the construction industry which had limited the opportunity they had to build, it was clear that younger architects, many of them with attitudes and ideas which matched the needs of the new Thatcherite world, were simply not being listened to.

With all their published work, Stiff + Trevillion were certainly part of the ongoing debate which now centred around two camps: the late modernists and the postmodernists. But they did not really see themselves as falling into either camp in such a starkly polarised way. Certainly their major built project was conservative but to their minds it was not 'styled' in any particular way. To them, Wateringbury

had developed in comfortable relationship to the existing eighteenth century house, using a faintly Classical form which was at the same time contemporary, in the spirit of Louis Kahn's Yale Center for British Art. They firmly believed that architecture should essentially be a response to the site and they vowed to do what was appropriate in those terms. In the accepted sense of the word, their work was 'contemporary', 'of its age', therefore, it was modern but with a small 'm'. As far as stark categorisations went, if called upon to design something '*moderne*' they knew they could do it but only if they felt it was appropriate.

In 1988, a re-run of 40 under 40 was commissioned. For Stiff + Trevillion, the timing was perfect, they were young, reasonably well known and had a substantial built project to their name. Being only too aware of the enormous potential for publicity, which the exhibition could generate, they went all out to submit a beautifully composed, expertly rendered panel in the best Dalibor Vesely style, which focused primarily on Wateringbury. Both in terms of its scale, its richness and its evidence of a comparatively large successfully completed commission, their presentation blew most of the other 600 odd submissions out of the water. While there may have been some useful 'politic-ing' taking place on their behalf behind the scenes from the likes of Peter Murray and 40 under 40 assessor David Rock, even today at a distance of 25 years, the presentation appears comprehensive and engaging, definitely good enough to win them a place in the final 40 exhibited schemes on merit alone.

Robert Venturi and Denise Scott-Brown designed The Sainsbury Wing at the National Gallery in Trafalgar Square—a notable example of postmodern design, 1991.

In his assessor's report, the renowned American architect Robert Stern, referring to the original 40 under 40 exhibition in New York in 1966, organised with a similar belief that something new was happening at the time, had stated with characteristic hyperbole that these new architects would, "rearrange the constellation of stars in the aesthetic firmament".

Fellow assessor, Peter Cook of Archigram fame was more grounded in his comments and from the exhibits identified four new theoretical groups. The first was what he called the "nostalgia camp", "intent on creating a red brick Merrie England with memories of Butterworth and Victorian engine sheds". The second group was mainly rationalist, heavily influenced by Foster, Rogers and Grimshaw's engineering styles, many of whom they had worked for previously. The third group was "obviously steeped in the Berlin and Irish proto-rationalist camp". Finally, according to Cook, the most inventive group fell into the category of historicism, "by which an interesting young architect is able to experiment on an interior space... and can use colours other than terracotta and buff. Sometimes they become mere exercises in the intelligent use of catalogues of Italian furniture and very occasionally a too-clever-by-half bit of geometry, but rather this than the nostalgia".[10]

Stiff + Trevillion's work definitely fell into this last category. They didn't see themselves as allied with either the nostalgia brigade or the rationalists. Over the last 25 years the partners have been completely disillusioned to witness how the Merrie England style has been adopted almost wholesale for the redevelopment of the UK throughout the provinces, except perhaps in a few protected cities such as Bath and Edinburgh. From Chesterfield in the north to Felixstowe in the south, every provincial town boasts an Ibis hotel designed in the same identical style, Butterworth-esque, a travesty to that great architect's memory. On the other hand, the hard 9H style of the rationalists, soaked in theory and unyielding certainty, was always equally unappealing to them. The sort of late-modern Meccano aesthetic adopted with alacrity for many of the new iconic commissions like Rogers' Lloyds Building in the City and Norman Foster's Sainsbury Centre at the University of East Anglia, for a contextualist like Mike it was all too simplistic, costly and impractical. He was determined not to permit this approach to replace the previous outdated architectural dogma.

Although this new classicism had undoubtedly hastened change, the politics of the movement had been muddied by the ferocious and very public intervention of Prince Charles and his classical revival supporters, the so-called "old fogies". Among the more successful classicist works, Venturi pulled off a triumph in Trafalgar Square and at Richmond-upon-Thames the erudite Quinlan Terry's popular riverside urban quarter was completed in 1992 and proved popular with the public and critics alike. However, Berthold Lubetkin, at the time a returning hero of the Modern Movement, stated in no uncertain terms that when he had been a student of architecture studying under Auguste Perret in 1924, "they had understood classicism as a humanist discipline rather than as a form of cladding" but for many architects who visit the Richmond development it is the lack of any meaningful relationship between facade and plan which is problematic, with modern, horizontal open-plan office floors set behind a series of individual Georgian-style house facades articulated in the vertical.[11] To the *cognoscenti* somehow it seems dishonest, yet public opinion has labelled it as one of the most popular 'Prince Charles-inspired' schemes and it has proved very successful commercially. Other less skilled exponents soon jumped on the bandwagon, building clumsy versions of the new classicism with projects such as the Queen's Gallery extension at Buckingham Palace (a slice of 'wedding cake' architecture, which in expressive power calls to mind the Fascist architecture of Troost in pre-war Munich). Although the urban plan for the redevelopment of Paternoster Square around St Paul's Cathedral was based on the original street pattern, neatly framing views of the dome in best historicist form, there are also some awful Disney-esque touches of appalling kitsch, including the main framing block to St Paul's along the left hand side of the entrance piazza.

Of the practices or individuals who were selected for 40 under 40 in 1988, almost every one of them went on to become well-known for contemporary urban architecture of the highest quality, perhaps not 'starchitects' in the league of Zaha Hadid or Daniel Libeskind but nevertheless firmly in the vanguard of a new generation of reformed modernists, names like David Chipperfield, Allies and Morrison, Fielden-Clegg-Bradley, Rab Bennets, Weston and Williamson, Trevor Horne, Sauerbruch-Hutton. And that selection process has stood the test of time, furnishing a new critical mass, which has helped fill the void between the mediocrity of commercial modernism and the equally moribund Neoclassicism of Prince Charles. Their work has led the way for subsequent commercial but distinctly design-led architects such as Allford Hall Monaghan Morris, Caruso St John and Sergison Bates, architects representing the new establishment but, unlike their predecessors, theirs is an architecture which is truly of its time, which resonates.

For Stiff + Trevillion, probably the most important by-product of the exhibition was the birth of an informal club of pluralist architects, which formed organically around the event. These relationships have since grown to become long standing professional friendships which have influenced the partners to learn and grow beyond the narrow confines of their initial prejudices and enthusiasms as graduates and which over the decades have also proved important in terms of mutual recommendations, which have led to important and lucrative commissions. They were now up there with the new establishment—Stiff + Trevillion had arrived.

SURVIVING THE NEXT RECESSION

Over the ensuing decade projects carried on coming in thick and fast and the practice rapidly out-grew its premises in the Colwyn-Foulkes shared space opposite the Commonwealth Institute in Kensington. Feeling more

ABOVE 40 under 40 exhibition catalogue cover and feature, 1988.

OPPOSITE TOP A residential scheme in Highgate, designed by Andy Trevillion and Bill Greensmith, his friend from their school days in St John's Wood. Unbuilt project commissioned by contractors John Murphy, 1989.

OPPOSITE BOTTOM High Street Kensington, interior of the main drawing studio, design in the pre-digital age.

confident in the light of their now flourishing reputation, they took-on their own office lease, a more centrally located unit above Kensington Market, opposite Church Street and Barkers. The practice soon grew from the two founding partners to employ a total of 15 people, including Mike's brother, Andrew Stiff, and a new partner, Richard Blandy.

At this time Stiff + Trevillion completed a number of residential projects and a large office development called KBBC in High Wycombe on behalf of the old Post Office Pension Fund (POSTEL), one of John Stiff's long-standing contacts. The project revolved around transforming what was essentially a bunch of industrial-style sheds which the partners set-about giving some sort of architectural order in the form of new cladding and landscaping. More importantly, this was their first design-and-build contract and as such helped them learn to deal with contractors in a more collegiate way, to function as a collaborative team rather than taking up competitive, adversarial positions. Bill Greensmith, an old friend from college joined the practice from architects Rick Mather and became Project Architect on the High Wycombe scheme.

Despite their relative success at Wateringbury and High Wycombe other projects which the practice took on were to prove much more problematic. According to Mike Stiff, the level of expectation and design commitment is greater at this stage in the developing career

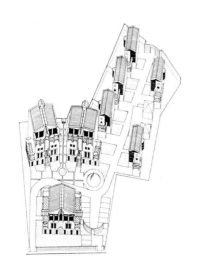

of an aspiring architect than at any other time. "Each project becomes the most important job in the office, consequently it becomes saturated with ideas. It is only later that the maturity, the 10,000 hours, gives you the surety and expertise to refine and condense a project, giving it the correct balance of the contemporary and the future proof", he says. The practice was still woefully short of systematic practice management know-how and confrontation, rather than collaboration, had been the main lesson learned about working with contractors from their college days. To be fair, co-operation and trust between architectural firms and construction teams was rare in those days and collaborative ways of working were frequently seen as a weakness—disputes with contractors were commonplace and over-spending had become the rule rather than the exception. Stiff remembers that contractors often took advantage of their relative inexperience and tended to bully. Partner meetings took place in the cordial but casual environment of The Britannia pub after work and although there was an energy and freedom to the projects there was little careful business planning. Consultant Stiff senior already had one eye on his retirement and was not always there to mentor the young partners.

At the peak of the Thatcher-Lawson boom, Stiff + Trevillion, always on the look-out for interesting new commissions, chanced on a new client by way of a rather rowdy Christmas drinks evening in The Brit. Keen to network, Andy started chatting to a group of well-oiled city guys in the public bar—clearly they were property boys. One was Richard Draycott a larger-than-life local character who had worked for the commercial surveying practice Richard Ellis and was now a property developer in his own right. As Andy bought the drinks, Mike was busy handing out their business cards. The night progressed, the drinks flowed freely and the camaraderie blossomed between them to such a rowdy, raucous pitch that the barman was eventually forced to ask them to leave. In the wake of this inebriated evening Andy received a call from his new chum Draycott with a request for them to look at a potential development site. Suddenly they had a new client.

Draycott was a hard-drinking giant of a man, who became a friend as much as a client. His flat in St John's Wood was designed by Stiff + Trevillion with the technically challenging brief to provide a bath for him and several female companions. Reinforced concrete was the only solution but Draycott was well pleased with the results. This was the beginning of a friendship that would eventually lead to a major commission to design and build a new office building in Egham in the 1990s (see chapter 3).

It was during this period of relative prosperity that both Mike and Andy felt the pressure to settle-down in their private lives and both of them got married. Coincidentally their wives were sisters which cemented their friendship and business partnership further. Both men also now bought homes for the first time, took on mortgages, started families. They had set-up in practice as mates and the business had been their shared interest, their baby. Now, however, they had real children to look after and personal responsibilities. These shared personal experiences tied them closer together like brothers in arms.

Then almost overnight, the phones stopped ringing. It was 1990 and a massive recession hit the British economy as a result of Black Monday in 1987. Interest rates were hiked up to a peak of 25 per cent in order to prevent a run on the pound, all to no avail—Britain was to be ejected from the International Monetary Fund. Stiff + Trevillion extended their overdraft in the belief that this situation would only last for a month or two. Their financial advisors assured them the trouble would pass and that everything would return to normality very soon. They watched as the projects they had in hand ground to a halt. They held out for another three months until they couldn't borrow any more and the bank called in their overdraft. Things were looking serious.

Ruefully Mike recalled a piece of advice from his former boss David Rock, "the minute you think you should make someone redundant, do it.... Act quickly." Unfortunately they were inexperienced in these matters, reluctant not to support their employees and they waited too long. By July the practice overdraft stood at £250,000. Coupled with the borrowing on the Italian property, this meant they owed over £400,000. They had guaranteed their borrowing using their own properties as security (in those days you had to vouch for such a sizeable loan personally). They were now staring bankruptcy in the face and the possibility of losing their family homes was very real.

In sheer desperation, Mike sold his office car to cover the rent, which was two months in arrears. However, this was not enough, so he traded in Andy's car whilst his partner was away on holiday. Apart from good will, these were really the only assets they had to show after eight years in practice, they were still not even managing to cover the service charges on the office space in Kensington. One morning they arrived to find that the locks had been changed and access was barred. There was a letter

from the landlord stuck to the door stating that they could not get back in until the debt was settled and that the bailiffs had been called. In these pre-mobile phone days they had to go across the road to an old red public phone box in order to call their solicitor.

As everything was locked and legal proceedings were pending, for a couple of spine-chilling days, they couldn't even invoice for the jobs they had completed. What was worse, according to the terms of the lease they had signed, it appeared that they had put up their own residential properties as surety against the lease. If they chose to, the bank could take their homes away to cover the debt. For both of the men with young families to provide for, it was a sobering prospect. This series of traumatic events that brought them so close to losing control of all that they had worked so hard for since setting up in practice, had a lasting effect on Stiff + Trevillion, changing their attitude to the business irrevocably. For the next ten years they would become paragons of caution and diffidence, consolidating their positions, refusing to stick their necks out even on occasions when perhaps it would have been opportune to do so.

Fortunately, they had an able and experienced solicitor who spotted a loophole in the contract, which showed that the landlord had in fact ended the lease on their offices. Not only did this remove the necessity of personal guarantees, it meant that for the leaseholder it would actually be preferable to have Stiff + Trevillion in residence than to leave the office empty. Soon the partners realised that they could negotiate a new lease on better terms, which would be more sustainable in those recessionary times. They then took the painful decision to reduce their staff to a bare minimum, a solemn, difficult task. But they felt that if they were to survive as a business they really had no choice. Both men recall vividly how bad they felt that week as they watched some great friends and committed, talented architects disappear from the practice.

Now Mike and Andy, Richard Blandy and Andy Stiff, together with one secretary, soldiered on, showing a resolute face to the world. They sub-let parts of the office to others (including Doug Clelland from their PCL days) and took-on any work they could find no matter how small the fee. John Stiff retired deciding that he no longer had the stomach for the fight. Stiff + Trevillion agreed to transfer the freehold of the Italian property to him on the understanding that he would dispose of it in order to clear part of the debt. However, even factoring this into the equation they still owed the bank £250,000 and still no work was coming in.

Thankfully, they managed to strike a deal with Barclays. The bank would cover their mortgages for a time, and give them time to pay off their debts, but in the meantime they were each permitted to withdraw just £100 a week to live on. This austerity was reflected back onto their domestic situations—they let out rooms in their houses and bought bicycles to travel to work, instead of flash cars. As there was little income from their existing client base in the UK, they started looking abroad for work. After a time an opportunity came up to do a limited competition in Berlin with their former tutor Doug Clelland. It was a long shot. New partner Richard Blandy was starting to seriously question his recent commitment to Stiff + Trevillion—what had he got himself into?

OVERLEAF Mike Stiff
drawing of a residential building
in St Petersburg, Russia.

— "Equal stakes, equal equity" makes sense in a risky partnership. During their tie-in with the John Stiff Partnership this was not the case and it caused problems.

— The economy is cyclical, the market for work is fickle, when the flow of commissions dries-up, get your cost base down immediately, don't wait until the debt is too great to manage.

— Employ a business mentor during the early years to take some of the uncertainty out of everyday business decisions.

— Study trips help to replenish the 'memory attic'— architecture is more of a vocation than most people realise.

— Whilst the business is important, take pride in every project.

— Your legal and financial consultants are critical, choose good ones that you trust and stick with them.

— Collaboration is at the heart of architecture. Form creative relationships with clients and contractors.

— Networking, particularly during the early years remains critically important, never forget it.

— When work is looking slow, do not wait to reduce the costs, act quickly and decisively.

CHAPTER 2 NOTES

1. Leslie Martin was the 1953 Deputy Chief Architect to the London County Council and led the Royal Festival Hall design team.

2. The New York Five were Peter Eisenman, Michael Graves, Charles Gwathmey, John Hedjuk and Richard Meier. Oxford University Press published *Five Architects* in 1975; The United Nations Secretariat Building, 1952, by Oscar Niemeyer and Le Corbusier.

3. Sherlock Holmes: "consider that a man's brain is an empty attic… a fool takes in all the lumber of every sort… so that the knowledge that might be useful to him is crowded out", from *A Study in Scarlet* by Arthur Conan Doyle.

4. *Civilisation*; 13-part series on BBC2, narrated by Kenneth Clark (1903–1983), 1969; also a book Clark, Kenneth, *Civilisation: a personal view*, London: John Murray, 2005.

5. Monica Pidgeon was the doyenne of post-war international architectural publishers. She became Editor of *Architectural Design* in 1946, turning it into essential reading for architects in practice. She retired in 1970 and was made a Fellow of the RIBA and an Honorary Fellow of the Architectural Association in 1979. Her work interviewing architects (Pidgeon Audio Visual), earned her an Honorary Fellowship of the American Institute of Architects in 1987.

6. *Architectural Design*, LA special.

7. *Blueprint* shared space with the 9H Gallery at 26 Cramer Street in Marylebone, London, W1, established by Ricky Burdett and Wilfried Wang (with financial support from Stewart Lipton). It was called 9H because they were hard-edged like a 9H pencil. According to Peter Murray, Cramer Street was a major crucible of the changing design consciousness, housing people such as Sebastian Conran, Burdett, Sudjic, David Chipperfield, Rowan Moore, Esterson, Tim Marlow, Nick Barley, Jan Abrahams, Luke Hayman et al.

8. In conversation with the author. Peter Murray is the Chairman of the charity Article 25, which promotes educational construction projects in the developing world.

9. "It is the prize no one wants to win. Six architectural firms will be sweating this week as they wait to hear on Friday whether their building has won the 2013 Carbuncle Cup, the award bestowed on Britain's ugliest buildings" in "Hated buildings are lined up for carbuncle Cup", *The Independent on Sunday*, 25 August 2013, p. 21.

10. 40 under 40 catalogue, RIBA Events, 1988, p. 1.

12. "Lubetkin was among the few who dared to suggest that behind his (The Prince's) critique the Royal survival instinct was at work—an impulse (consciously or otherwise) to align popular taste with the monarchy, conflate conservation with nostalgia and thus objectively maintain a larger status quo" in Allan, John, *Berthold Lubetkin: Architecture a Tradition of Progress*, London: Artifice books on architecture, 2013, p. 575; Perret was deeply rooted in the Beaux Arts tradition. By studying under him, as had Le Corbusier a generation earlier; they had in effect made contact with the tradition of French Rationalism stretching back to Viollet-le-Duc and the mid-nineteenth century. Allan, John, *Berthold Lubetkin* p. 576.

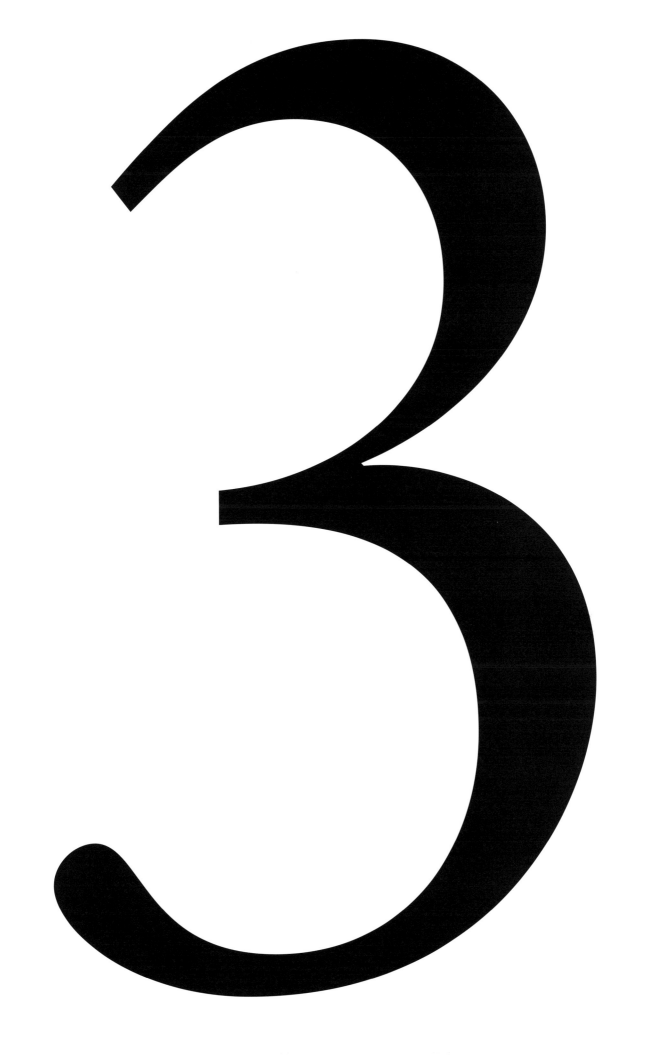

The 1990s

RECESSION AND RECOVERY

The recession had been so severe that only a paper-thin layer of funds remained in reserve to save Stiff + Trevillion from financial ruin as they faced soaring interest rates on the repayments they had to make on all they had borrowed. What are the lessons Stiff + Trevillion learned from the events of 1990 and how did they manage to hold things together in the face of such severe economic difficulties? How do you decide whether it's time to walk away from a business where circumstances have brought you and your family so close to disaster, or to hold fast and tough it out?

Faced with the prospect of paying back £250,000 there were only two options; the partners could enter into a voluntary arrangement, whereby the creditors were reimbursed at an agreed rate (after any assets had been liquidated), or they could try and battle it out and clear the debt gradually. The former option would almost certainly have forced the sale of their homes, so they chose the latter.

To do this it was important to ensure that the business could earn enough to pay its way back to safety. They came to an agreement with the bank that both their monthly mortgage payments would be covered and that they could retain three paid members of staff and cover the monthly rent for the office premises. In return they conceded that anything they earned over and above the sum needed to cover these outgoings would go straight back to the bank. The two partners were each permitted to draw £100 a week to live on which meant that they were effectively earning less than their PA. However, they realised that until the business was free of debt it would be impossible for it to grow again. Day-to-day survival must be enough for the moment; if they could keep their heads down and get through this period of austerity they hoped the practice would eventually start to recover.

There was, for a time, a monastic feel to their lives, and this inevitably created stresses and tensions in family life. For their wives, now forced to pull the family purse strings tight, it was an enormous challenge. Whilst they all recognised that the recovery of the architectural practice was central to their collective well-being, there was also a sense that they needed to pull together. In particular, Sara Trevillion, Andy's wife, became his rock during this particular storm. Her strength of character and understanding were central to Andy's ability to hold his nerve despite the financial difficulties, giving him invaluable stability and perspective.

During the early years of the decade, the risk to their partnership was considerable. There were many quiet moments when both men felt the situation could not go on, tempting offers from commercial practices drifted in and tough sacrifices had to be made. Stiff recognises now that in a way they were manacled together by the debt, an umbilical cord that in hindsight probably strengthened their partnership. The prospect of working for someone else was not only impractical because of their financial obligations, it was also unappealing for the two young architects having tasted the joys of creative independence. For Mike in particular it was an impossibility, working with Trevillion had always given him the creative freedom he needed as a high-energy artistic personality, and provided the solidity and quiet confidence he needed as a foil to his impulsive ways.

Dissolving the practice was discussed but Andy was resolute and wise. He believed that what had happened was an essential part of the learning experience, they must pay-off their debts and move forward again together, older, wiser and more resilient. Reflecting on those days, Mike now realises how important Andy's role was in stabilising the situation and fostering the subsequent recovery of the practice. Left to himself his own inclination was to panic and make critical decisions on an emotional basis rather than a rational one. Overwhelmed by the troubles, he had the capacity to cast to the winds all that they had built-up during the 1980s, and on a number of occasions it was Andy who pulled him back from the brink. But this dynamic, though often fraught, made their partnership strong; after these events, there would never again be insecurities or misunderstandings between the two.

By keeping their problems quiet, their heads down and their debts under control, the reputation of the practice remained untarnished. By Christmas 1990 work had slowly started to trickle in again, a couple of house extensions and a small apartment refurbishment, however certainly not profitable enough to make significant in-roads into the debt. No matter how much positive publicity these designs received, and it was surprising how persuasive a Stiff rendering could make even the smallest, most insignificant project, there was no getting away from the scary prospect of them remaining on this breadline for decades. A fierce recession was still gripping the UK and times were tough. They desperately needed a big commission to break through to the next level. In addition there were now three families to feed.

BLANDY JOINS THE PRACTICE

Richard Blandy's route into a partnership with Stiff + Trevillion was typical of the coincidental ways in which the business was organically developing. The partners were learning on the job, acquiring their business acumen by dealing with the issues as they arrived. Recruitment, for example, was an area in which Stiff + Trevillion continued to trust their instincts and preferences, there was no agency headhunting of appropriately qualified professionals. Paper qualifications were all very well but they knew how wildly imaginative written resumes could be, especially at a time when decent jobs in the profession were hard to come by. Rather they preferred to check out what experience and expertise was available in their immediate orbit among trusted friends, ex-colleagues, relations, friends of friends. Any prospective employee had to be relaxed yet sharp, completely trustworthy and above all there had to be chemistry. Of course you must be canny, there are always bad apples, but Stiff + Trevillion believed in the idea that friends tend to be more reliable and loyal. Personal recommendations were then followed-up by checks into the person's inherent judgement, which might determine how the three would gel. They didn't always get it right, but mostly they did.

Richard's decision to stay with the practice in the wake of the 1990 crash, cemented the relationship further. He may have thought twice about this decision however, when it was staring at bankruptcy a year later. When the enormity of their situation finally hit Mike and Andy and they realised they would have to let some of their people go if they were to survive, one of the first conversations they had centred on Richard's further involvement. He was not a partner, he could simply walk away if he wanted to, but among all of the employees they had relied on he was their favourite on many levels and they were very loathe to lose him. They hoped that despite the myriad difficulties he would decide to stay on, but suspected he would not. Rather to their surprise, and delight, Richard stated decisively that he was there for the duration and wanted to be part of the long term plans of Stiff + Trevillion, there was absolutely no question of him walking. However, in order to consolidate his position he wanted a profit share, he needed a partnership. At that moment the two architects felt it wasn't much to give away. They agreed.

For Richard, the attraction of Stiff + Trevillion was two-fold. On one side he had been impressed by their handling of the practice's difficulties and by their courage under fire. They had held fast during the darkest moments, no easy feat in those recession-ridden times. On the other, he realised that, having just been admitted to the 40 under 40 club, it was clear these boys were going places. Mike was obviously very talented and Andy was good with clients and, in the professional environment, the perfect foil for Mike's sometimes wayward 'artistic' temperament—he liked them.

Blandy came from an artistic background himself, (his older brother is a professional artist), but was of a more scientific bent. His motivation was similar to Mike and Andy's, he wanted to get-on, to make a healthy living doing what he enjoyed most, in his case running jobs and building. In addition it was important to him to retain his moral and creative self-respect. He didn't want to work on projects that risked being nominated for the Carbuncle Cup. He felt that Stiff, although relatively young, was quick, decisive and sure (unlike many artistic temperaments always in need of time for experimentation), and operated like a businessman when he needed to, instinctively designing to the technical level appropriate for the budget. To Richard he was that rare animal, an artist who was absolutely resolute when it came to quality but who was also efficient in process—Mike could always hit a deadline. He noticed how dedicated Mike was, often alone working up until the small hours if a project was required for presentation the next day. Blandy saw that he had drive, commitment and talent and for these qualities he deeply respected and admired the young architect.

In the area of project management Richard Blandy was meticulous with a systematic approach to the task of controlling costs and maintaining quality that brought a new rigour to the practice. He didn't see the work involved in running a job as a grind, he enjoyed focussing on the detail and was unfazed by the stress and responsibility of budgets and deadlines. The office for Richard was a place of certainty where he felt competent, somewhere he could invest all of his concentration on the task in hand; it was almost a form of therapy. This sense of pleasure in the task of building, communicated itself to the clients, particularly the commercial surveyors and high-end estate agents they were now trying to woo. Unlike Mike and Andy, Richard had a faintly patrician air which had rubbed-off on him during his public school education. He looked the part and clients felt he was more a part of the 'old boy' network than either Mike or Andy could ever be. In the post-meltdown period of Stiff + Trevillion's slow renaissance, Blandy was definitely a positive influence.

During this period when they had to take on any work they could find, living very much hand-to-mouth, Richard Blandy's family was largely supported by his wife's endeavours. Sophy was resolute and resourceful. Richard had worked hard to convince her that everything would come right in the end, taking pains to explain why he had decided to throw his lot in with this particular crew. "I either hang around at Stiff + Trevillion and get a profit share, or I set-up on my own", he told her, but why risk going off on his own when the work with Mike and Andy complemented his own skills so well? Richard was committed to the practice and it was clear to Mike and Andy that his loyalty should be rewarded by being made an equity partner when the finances stabilised. Sophy breathed

a sigh of relief—her trust in Richard was justified and it seemed their sacrifices were starting to pay off.

Then towards the end of 1992 a couple of substantial projects emerged for the practice. On the back of 40 under 40, Stiff + Trevillion had been placed on a list of prospective consultants for the refurbishment and extension of a large house in Holland Park. The client was Jeremy Lloyd who was the property director at HSBC. Richard attended the first interview with Andy. They were up against some strong competition, however by this time their portfolio was comprehensive. They showed Wateringbury, and a couple of other largish commercial projects from the John Stiff stable, to provide evidence of their accomplished design skills. There was also a decent selection of refurbishment projects accompanied by impressive written testimonials. Not all of this work had been very profitable for the firm but to Jeremy Lloyd it was clear that they had considerable talent and had provided a comprehensive service.

Jeremy Lloyd was a man suspicious of the term "professionals", with a tendency to view architects as airy-fairy lightweights with no idea about the bottom line. He didn't suffer fools gladly. Intuitively, Andy felt that they needed to persuade the client they were of his tribe. They agreed that if most of the questions were directed to the public-school educated Blandy then Trevillion should remain quiet, and vice versa. They would rely on their intuition to decide how best to play it.

Devising this strategy enabled Trevillion to go to the meeting feeling confident and well prepared. Sure enough, Richard held most of the interview, fielding the technical questions. Halfway through however the prospective client asked about Andy's status, was this guy really an architect? If so, where was his cut-glass home counties accent and 'eccentric' bow tie? The absence of the stereotypical architect was obviously perplexing to Lloyd, it was also intriguing. Andy's apparent lack of polish, his steady pragmatic demeanour and no-nonsense approach put the team in a positive light. Sitting alone in the studio the previous weekend, Andy had rehearsed the questions that he imagined might be asked. Every objection had been anticipated, every query resolved. His replies were clear, confident and to the point.

Lloyd hit it off with Blandy and Trevillion immediately; they were speaking the same language. It was a winning performance in which nothing had been left to chance and by the end of the appointment a very beneficial relationship had been forged. Aside from their portfolio, the balance of Richard's job-running knowledge and Andy's worldly integrity probably did the trick.

The commission was on the face of it another Wateringbury, however this time they were working for a much more exacting client. Every drawing and detail was meticulously checked and debated, revised, checked again and then finally presented to the client for sign-off. It was dependent on Blandy's running things from beginning to end and being committed to

Lansdowne Road, London, a large house refurbishment and extension for Jeremy Lloyd and family, one of the first significant, projects of the early 1990s, which helped to establish the practice's identity in west London, 1993.

the project full time. The house was completely refurbished with 40 per cent volume added on in the form of various extensions. There was also a swimming pool installed in the extended basement. The project entailed complicated interior finishes and seamless joinery to make it appear as though old was melting into new. They needed to achieve what the client envisioned, refining it as they went and still remaining within budget. This honed Richard's skills and established the work ethos that remains at the heart of his process to this day.

Although the project took longer than anticipated, the brief was consistent and the budget robust. Blandy was on-site for two years, completely dedicated, and on many occasions acting above and beyond the call of duty. He showed roofing contractors how to form the lead drips he required for the parapet details, he demonstrated the way they wanted the timber grain to run on the new stair cupboards. Once the client had finally taken up residence in his new home, he personally went round to fire-up the heating system one Sunday when the sub-contractor was unavailable. This total focus on client care, a real test of their professionalism at the time, was to become key to Stiff + Trevillion's reputation. Blandy had been pivotal in all that they had set out to achieve with this important client and the success of the project was to lead onto another larger project that would eventually help to secure the practice.

BERLIN AND THE UNIFICATION

In 1990, seemingly out of nowhere, a serendipitous opportunity arose for Stiff + Trevillion. The German colleague of one of John Stiff's former partners was looking towards East Berlin and considering transferring his professional focus there. He had secured a deal to develop an old Soviet air-base situated on the edge of a village between Berlin and the Polish border but he needed help to execute the project. He checked

LEFT Pencil and crayon rendering by Mike Stiff, 1992, the entrance to an apartment block showing war-time shrapnel damage, both partially drawn on-site in the east Berlin district of Mitte.

RIGHT The Berlin Wall viewed from the west across what remained of Alexander Platz, 1990.

out Mike and Andy's work, asked around, received positive feedback. Contact was made with them and a meeting set-up. They got along well with the older man and agreed to take it on. Mike was rather uneasy, to him it felt like a long shot, but Andy recognised the potential and encouraged the venture. They were working for a modest fee, woefully inadequate to compensate them for all the time and energy required on such a complex project and with this challenging client. However, Andy was convinced this would be an investment for their future and wooed his partner with the notion that the project had an important element of historicism in it too, an undertone of revealing and reanimating the past that was fascinating and somehow noble. This might be a way to a greater understanding of the long-obscured, often sinister mysteries of life behind the Iron Curtain. Mike was hooked and fired-up once they agreed to take on the project. The challenges of working in a foreign land where they didn't speak the language and knew virtually no one didn't deter them one jot.

Political events at this time were about to turn the city of Berlin into one vast building site. It had been divided since 1945 as part of the settlement between Communist Russia and the West. There was of course a physical separation, the Wall, which was an arbitrary line cutting through what had once been a single, vibrant, pre-war city.

The divide was in the form—two low concrete walls running parallel and an area of open ground, the so-called "no man's land", between. This middle ground was intensively surveyed by East German security guards from their elevated machine gun towers, briefed to shoot down any escapees from the Communist side. Nobody tried to escape in the other direction except in a coffin.

To get to the city from mainland west Germany in the 1990s, you either took a heavily guarded train through the Russian-controlled land, which surrounded Berlin, or drove your car through a fenced-off motorway corridor. Once there you could take a day trip across the border to East Berlin, passing through Checkpoint Charlie, the heavily fortified street barrier made famous in Len Deighton's novels and iconic 1960s spy films such as *Funeral in Berlin*. Living inside the Communist Bloc made acute paranoia the normal state of mind for many of its citizens, understandably so. For the few tourists willing to deal with all the bureaucratic difficulties, it was alien, sinister, dangerous but strangely romantic.

Even 40 years after the cessation of hostilities the East Berlin cityscape was still characterised by bomb sites and poorly repaired buildings, visibly pock-marked with bullet holes and shrapnel, vivid reminders for visitors of the painful retribution its citizens had suffered towards the end of the Second World War and of the poverty and cultural isolation of the Cold War era which followed. The divided continent that came to vivid focus in the fractured city of Berlin, seemed like a permanent, immutable condition of post-war Europe. When Mike had travelled there to deliver their IBA competition entry in 1982, it seemed inconceivable to imagine that they would be back for work less than a decade later.[1]

It was in June 1979 that John Paul II, who had been elected to the papacy the previous autumn, returned to his Polish homeland for a nine day visit that had unforeseen consequences. As part of the post-war settlement, Poland, like East Germany, had been a Russian satellite for decades, but the Pope's visit gave his long demoralised compatriots fresh impetus to resist Moscow's control. John Paul's visit paved the way for the rise of the independent Solidarity Trade Union in 1980, a development that played a crucial role in the demolition of Soviet rule in Eastern Europe a decade later.

Towards the end of the decade the Eastern Bloc began to fall apart as the peaceful revolution gathered momentum.[2] First, the border between Hungary and Austria was breached; this was followed domino-like by Bulgaria, Czechoslovakia, Romania and East Germany which in turn precipitated the fall of Communism in Russia itself. The Berlin Wall officially remained guarded after 9 November 1989, but in effect the inter-German border had become meaningless weeks before.

On 3 October 1990, amid warnings that it would take years to rebuild the shattered economy, the necessary two-thirds majority of deputies in the East German parliament formally agreed to unification with West Germany. It was greeted with a mixture of relief and joy by politicians from all parties in West Germany, the end of months of uncertainty, giving a fresh impetus for private investment in the newly unified city.

The events of 3 October precipitated the campaign for the first all-German democratic elections in nearly 60 years, under a single electoral system now approved by both parliaments. Chancellor Kohl, greeting the Volkskammer's decision as "a day of joy", tried to raise Germans' sights above the disputes, particularly those relating to the cost of revitalising the failed Communist state. On the day of the election he declared that the process of unification was "unprecedented in the history of post-war Europe". It was taking place without war, bloody revolution or force and in full agreement with Germany's friends and neighbours in the West and in the East, a triumph of diplomacy and political will.[3]

With bleak economic prospects in the UK, some intrepid investors and developers were already looking towards the Eastern Bloc and to Berlin in particular. Over the following ten years it would resume its role as the country's capital city with a restored parliament and legislature. The potential for redevelopment was boundless, the task of transforming an entire city-state of threadbare 1950s era building stock to something approaching contemporary architecture fit for the new millennium was inspiring some great new work. But finding a way in was not so straight-forward for foreign companies—during the early days of reunification trying to operate behind the breach in the Iron Curtain was still fraught.

For Stiff + Trevillion the commission would move quickly, assuming a distinctly surreal quality from beginning to end. In February 1990 the partners flew into Berlin Tegel. They were collected at the airport in a standard East Berlin issue Trabant, a Bakerlite bodied antique with a two-stroke oil-guzzling engine that emitted smoky exhaust fumes in continuation. Surrounded by all the pneumatic Mercs, BMWs and Audis at the airport, it looked anachronistic. These products of the latest Western technology, symbols of the successful post-war West German economy were all state-of-the-art. By comparison the Trabant, the best in economical automotive design that the Soviet's could produce during their 60 years of power, was a laughing stock, a sort of comedy car, graphically illustrating how far the Soviet economies had slipped behind those of the West. The Trabbie's suspension was also no match for the potholed roads in the East, Mike and Andy felt their fillings coming loose as they jolted into Mitte and back into the past.

That night they stayed in the Berolina hotel on the eastern edge of the old city. Their accommodation was classic Soviet style retro-modern. It was, recalls Stiff, almost hip but unintentionally so. Looking around it occurred to him that after all those years under Communism the East Germans had few design concepts of their own, mainly a sort of dated idea of modern architecture seemingly sourced from 1950s American comic books. Their hotel was comically modish too in its faded period costume but behind the functional facade hardly anything worked. The plumbing seemed to have an uncanny facility for either scalding hot water gushing into the antiquated roll top iron bath in a strange air-filled pumping motion, or dribbling icy-cold brownish puddles. The carpets were threadbare. Inside a rickety cupboard in their room the two found a chilling piece of graffiti, dated 1976. In awkward English it said, "Stayed here and the room suddenly filled with sewage, I will always remember my visit, long live the revolution!"

The next day they travelled towards the village of Diensdorf-Radlow, 15 minutes from the Polish border. The journey east was slow and uncomfortable, travelling along poorly maintained pre-war autobahns to land transport and troop planes.

The village itself was attractive but obviously under-developed. They arrived outside the town hall shortly after ten in the morning for their first meeting to be greeted by their diminutive Project Manager. The jovial Dr Guipel, dressed in a beige safari suit, was to them a caricature of the fashion conscious East German man-about-town. He spoke little English but could recite poems by Edgar Allen Poe by heart. His face had all the faux cosmopolitan suavity of a once-powerful man grappling with his recent somewhat melancholy decline. Clearly he had the ear of the Mayor and was well connected to the old regime. His team of local landowners, farmers and traders, were newly enriched by the exchange of one of

their East German marks, previously of little value, into two Western Marks. It was daylight bribery.

The meetings with the two British architects were always held in the Mayor's chambers on the first floor of the town hall building. The Mayor and his entourage were housed in a strangely dingy suite of rooms in various shades of brown and orange, which had formerly been shared with the local Stasi HQ. There were chicken coops around the ground floor entrance areas, feathers and the sound of unseen fluttering creatures seemed to mark their every arrival and passage through the entrance loggia as they headed for the shabby stairway. Above, on the second and third floors there were a couple of crumbling apartments. It powerfully evoked the Cold War in all its world-weary, down-at-heel detail.

Mike and Andy had been commissioned to develop a masterplan for the village as a whole and the more detailed design of extensions across the former air base. They proposed mixed developments of work and housing blocks, with sport, leisure and retail creating the public parts along Wilhelmstrasse lines (no churches were required). As the scheme evolved it would be presented in Radlow with the aid of a single squeaky slide projector and an elderly translator. Unfortunately he seemed to speak a pre-war form of 1930s schoolboy English that was not always nuanced enough to communicate difficult philosophical ideas. They tried to keep it

simple for their provincial audience, but how to explain Phenomenology and *The Art of Memory* to this bedraggled group?

What resulted was an intensive period of analysis and design work conceived in London with very little consultation. The team of locals found it hard to understand what was going on. It was as if they had never been consulted about anything ever before and if they now ventured to express a view it was always about something arbitrary or trivial—the colour of a door, the width of an entrance gate for a horse and cart, what they would do with all the derelict planes at the east end of the site. They never had an opinion about the new scheme that was being proposed but only seemed bent on preserving the status quo. When there were questions about the big things they waited for the nod from Guipel and his Mayor, then voted as one.

Stiff + Trevillion found the whole process extremely frustrating. The presentations were hard work and they had little idea of how much they were managing to communicate to the group via their ropey interpreter. Sometimes they thought the client group had got it only to be disappointed a few moments later realising that they were talking at cross-purposes. In one meeting when Trevillion had referred to Lenin, the former East Germans had assumed he was talking about John Lennon. It was long-winded, sometimes confrontational and often surreal.

On one occasion they were making steady progress when there was a loud, mournful wail from the room above which stopped them in their tracks. The agitated Mayor sent a clerk out to find out what was going on. His minion returned shortly and whispered to the Mayor, who signalled to Guipel in turn. Guipel immediately told Mike and Andy to complete their presentation, so in the dimly lit room with the squeaky projector

OPPOSITE Hotel Berolina in the centre of east Berlin, where Stiff + Trevillion stayed on their way to their first commission in post-unification Germany. With the Kino International and Bar Moscow in the foreground, where Stiff + Trevillion spent many a happy hour.

ABOVE View from the rear window of their chauffeur driven Trabant travelling from Berlin towards Frankfurt Oder to visit the site in Diensdorf-Radlow. This Cold War autobahn was designed without a central reservation so that in the event of an invasion from the West, Soviet troop planes could use it as a landing strip.

they ploughed on feeling a frisson of momentary danger at the unlikely situation. As the boys were leaving, they were surprised to see a stretcher with a body strapped to it, face covered by a grey blanket, being borne down the stairs just ahead of them by a pair of elderly medics who were pitching and swaying in a mildly inebriated syncopation. Andy stepped forward to lend a hand but was awkwardly received, his behaviour seeming out of place, too kindly and Western. What was being played out in front of them appeared to be nothing out of the ordinary however; everyone else was taking it nonchalantly. A sobbing woman now trailed morosely behind the little group, inconsolable. No one said anything. The entourage was escorted a safe distance down to the street where the stretcher was then slid into the back of an old Dacia estate car.

A policeman was officiously rubber-stamping forms on the roof of the car and handing copies to the woman. For these people they saw, Soviet era red tape was still as much an accepted part of everyday reality as it had been 50 years ago, the familiarity of the bureaucratic procedures almost comforting to them. It was the woman's 27 year-old son who had passed they finally learned, an alcoholic who had garroted himself, perhaps unable to comprehend the immense changes looming on the horizon with the approach of capitalist democracy. It was at least a quick and painless death.

To Mike and Andy, the scene seemed to encapsulate the depressing end of an era, rather than the optimistic beginning of a new one. They realised that for many millions of people across the newly democratised East, this peaceful revolution would actually come at a high price. There was not enough time to feed the individualistic message into such ideologically wired brains as these. They now needed to perform like small highly manoeuvrable speedboats. Instead they were tied to this juggernaut, a massive oil tanker of a state heading inexorably towards the sand banks, incapable of changing direction in time.

Predictably, the scheme went nowhere. The locals were just too ingrained in the inertia of state-sponsored Communism and suspicious of what they saw as a Western threat to their heroic culture and pragmatic morality. Land ownership was complex and would become even more so as the pre-war owners began to return to east Germany to stake claim on their families' property. There were too many people wanting to make a fast buck and Guipel no longer had the political muscle and necessary power of his Stasi hey-days to make it happen.

In some respects, they would be proved right, post-unification, the moral tone declined dramatically, the common purpose was replaced by... nothing very much. On the other hand, looking back to those times, it is interesting to note how a politician who grew up in the East, has transcended the political divide, bringing a certain gentle, low-key wisdom, combined with a hard-bitten unsentimental rationality to her role as Chancellor. A role which is effectively also the head of the new European state. Angela Merkel is Guipel in a trouser suit, the politician who puts all the other second-rate European leaders firmly in their place.

The masterplan drawing for Diensdorf-Radlow, a proposed development around an existing village and a disused Russian air-base in east Germany, following the unification of the country, 1990.

STABILISING THE RECOVERY

The unification of Berlin was to have profound long-term benefits for the economies of the European states. For developers with cash to invest and the necessary spirit of adventure there was serious money to be made. Doug Clelland, their tutor and mentor from the PCL days, had already anticipated this opportunity. He had been involved in the Berlin Building Exhibition (IBA) from 1980 and, following eight years of immersion, had developed something of an expertise in post-war reconstruction strategies for the city.[4] He had become an important guiding figure, a powerful spokesman for the new architecture, promoting his Dalibor Veseley-style urban philosophies, and had cultivated a number of important contacts in Berlin towards the end of the 1980s. Doug could also be very persuasive and now he wanted to build. He called Mike to relay some exciting news. He had taken office space in the Charlottenberg area and was completing a couple of IBA projects including a significant mixed-use, part-residential, part-social centre for the deaf. He was in the frame too for a new Siemens manufacturing building in the east Berlin hinterland.

He asked Stiff + Trevillion if they would like to contribute to the forthcoming presentation. The pitch was for a £25 million contract, which Clelland suggested, could be partly designed in London. He described the streamlined building process, a form of in-house design and build, which was, in terms of its contracting procedures, years ahead of what was then possible in the UK. In Germany it was made possible by the clear split between the creative and the technical architects. The contractors, stated Clelland with a typical rhetorical flourish, "turned up on site in white coats, looking like scientists".

The sketches of the scheme were strong but there was no doubt that a desire to look beyond borders, to find new talent and ideas, played a crucial part in the success of the pitch. Siemens recognised the significance of the moment and opted for something new. The building would be a celebration of the political and economic alignment of the emerging European Union, a central requirement for the reunification of the two Germanys. Treptow would be a building, which was totally at odds with the narrow pre-war nationalism, which had brought with it such anarchy and destruction to Germany. Its authors would be an international team of collaborators—Scottish, English and German.

Clelland, Stiff + Trevillion now set up a joint venture, CST Architekten, and within six months, the team was established in Berlin with an office and a large contract. This was a defining moment in the recovery of Stiff + Trevillion, the lifeline Mike and Andy had prayed for to keep the London operation going. Seven people were now working on the Treptow project in the UK with four more engaged on it in the Berlin office. And there was another piece of good news waiting in the wings. Impressed by their excellent work on his house, Jeremy Lloyd commissioned another sizeable job from the practice. It was for the refurbishment of four penthouses on an apartment block in Park Lane, which his bank HSBC had inherited as a bad debt from the infamous Polly Peck crash.[5] Fountain House already had planning consent but needed detailed design approvals. The partners now had enough fee-paying work to begin paying off chunks of their debt and to add a few more staff to the team. Stiff + Trevillion were finally beginning to see the light at the end of the tunnel.

It was good news but they weren't out of the woods yet. They still had the weight of the debt influencing their every move. Mike relocated to Berlin for the duration of the project living in a small flat there and returning home to London for brief weekend visits. Every other Friday evening after landing he would go straight from Heathrow to the office, meet Andy and Richard to debrief, then end-up in The Britannia for a couple of late convivial beers. The long absences began to place considerable strains on his marriage and on his family life. He arrived home exhausted where his wife and daughter expected his undivided attention but he was too tired, worried about the business and short of both time and good humour to respond. After lunch on Sunday he would be off to the airport again with a large roll of drawings under his arm.

Andy Trevillion meanwhile ran the London office, taking over responsibility for the finances, dealing with the bank and other creditors, fire fighting on a daily basis. Along with Richard Blandy he also helped to pitch for more work. Now they had a financial buffer and were able to be more selective and discerning in what they agreed to take-on. They avoided high-cost refurbishments for difficult clients, concentrating instead on more straight-forward projects with a good profit margin, or focussing on potential client leads; a developer's house or showroom for a major manufacturer.

They were now more battle-hardened, beginning to understand the business of architecture and where they wanted to be positioned within its diverse range of possibilities. Top priority was to diminish the burden of debt somehow. They were learning that they had to be more savvy in their choice of work, Stiff + Trevillion was not a charity; there was no room now for vanity projects.

BUILDING TREPTOW

The Berlin building was a big commission, a production facility with offices for WSSB, the company that provided signals and controls for most of the East European railway system. The brief was complicated further by the necessity of incorporating manufacturing, storage and office/research accommodation all in one compact block.

The Treptow facility was to be the first new building constructed in the east following the fall of Communism. Symbolically the site was on the line of the Berlin Wall where Easterners and Westerners had once looked across the deadly divide and observed each other from their respective living room windows, in contact visually but physically separated by a million ideological words and actions. Now the land was conjoined and the houses razed to make way for the vast new manufacturing facility.

ABOVE Treptow, Berlin, a new Siemens manufacturing HQ, designed by Clelland, Stiff + Trevillion, with Hartmut Eichhorn. Model made in wood by Richard Armiger in 1991, which avoided the ongoing debates around the colours and textures to be adopted for the facades.

OVERLEAF View of the internal courtyard, a raised garden with walls clad in white glazed brick, a reference to the traditional Berlin *hof*, 1993. The courtyard was an important sustainability devise, enabling passive ventilation to the interiors.

Berlin had traditionally been a liberal city and in the 1990s it was renewing its outward-looking perspective, awarding commissions to a number of foreign architects such as Norman Foster who designed the new German Parliament around the remains of the Reichstag, images of the gutted classical building in 1945 full of gloating Russian tank commanders, fresh in the collective memory. That perpetual traveller Daniel Liebeskind had also moved from London to Berlin where he was busy extending the old Berlin Museum into a stunning new piece, the Jewish Museum, which has since become one of the most iconic buildings in the city.

Siemens, the client company, had always viewed architecture as an essential reflection of its own corporate identity. During the pre-Nazi days of the 1930s they had adopted the progressive planning policies of the Modern Movement pioneers, adopting a progressive modernism for their model town adjacent to Tegel Airport—Siemenstadt had housing designed by the great organic designer, Hans Scharoun, amongst others.[6]

Siemens' Head of Architecture was now Professor Gunther Standke and he was the person to whom the CST partners now reported. A lot of the key Siemens preconditions were included in their brief, meaning that the team were expected to work within tight constraints, something which at times they found extremely frustrating, at others strangely comforting. Standke had worked for Richard Meier, and was well-versed in Meier's white modernist architecture and favoured this style. Doug and Mike on the other side viewed it as being essentially anti-historicist and too formal; design was like a complicated examination question you had to get right. Consequently there were many battles between the British colleagues and the Siemens gatekeeper, Standke.

The 25,000 square metre floor area embraced new sustainability ideas such as thermal mass, natural ventilation, solar control and green roofs,

all designed to avoid the necessity of air-conditioning. Central courtyard spaces ventilated the offices, and allowed daylight deep into the plan, to provide rooftop gardens and pleasant walkway promenades. It was to be an ocean liner of a building, enveloping all of the worker's needs, an expression perhaps of the newly united greater Germany.

The design team became well-versed in these novel sustainability strategies long before they became commonplace in the UK. For Mike it was an intensive education, which would pay handsome dividends when he returned to London in the mid-1990s. As well as this, the building assumed a studied urban discipline, a reinterpretation of Berlin's 22-metre-high traditional courtyard blocks. This was the city architect Hans Stimman's vision. He had decided that a critical reconstruction within these slightly arbitrary constraints would provide a controlled and coherent whole. The planners sincerely wished to avoid the muddled chaos of post-war reconstruction in cities like Liverpool and Coventry.

The urban strategy would eventually find architectural expression in new buildings by fashionable international names such as Rob Krier, Aldo Rossi and Peter Eisenman. It evolved as a discreet celebration of the city's history, an orthodoxy that arguably only a foreigner could propose in the wake of Nazism. For a city so besmirched by its past, it is perhaps surprising that historicism of this type would be so readily adopted as the basis for Berlin's overall post-Cold War reconstruction brief. Nevertheless it was this decision that was largely responsible for the look and feel of today's Berlin.

OPPOSITE Siemensstadt was constructed as worker's housing to service the nearby electrical factory, which employed 60,000 workers, 1929–1931.

ABOVE The Siemens HQ in Munich designed by Richard Meier. A white aesthetic expresses a unified global corporate brand, in contrast to the aims of the Treptow team, to make a richer architecture, which also reflects important local cultural influences.

It should be said that the CST design team informed the Treptow building with an over-complicated aesthetic. Four different elevations were developed which orientated to the four physical axis to which the site related, and this proved to be a little heavy-handed, an unnecessary piece of over-elaboration. In response to Siemens feedback Mike helped to play things down and make it more practical, while Gunther Standke did the rest imposing a technocratic grid and curtain wall system, which was applied across each facade. Mike recalls that in the end elements of elaboration were only permitted on corners and around entrances and in courtyards but beyond that, creativity was quite severely restricted.

Today, Treptow has a strange Shrek-like appearance, an amalgam of old and new, vivid and larger than life, not sitting altogether comfortably in its contained urban packaging. However, it is undeniably intense, brave, of its time. In addition to the advanced eco-technology, the main structural materials, steel and concrete, are combined within an ingenious structural system which literally slots together like scaled-up Lego bricks, avoiding the need to bolt or weld, another avant-garde idea at the time, which was subsequently adopted across the UK construction industry and used by Mike and Andy on a later Siemens commission in England as well.

Looking at the building now it is impossible for Mike not to recall through its lines all the creative blood, sweat and tears which went into its making, all those intense, late-night debates in a succession of Berlin bars between the two high-octane designers, Doug and himself, balanced by the cool pragmatism of their German colleague and lead architect, Hartmut Eichhorn. It was hard work for them all—intense, frenetic days followed by late nights, rivers of beer and *hausmannkost*, the typical German soul food which they all loved but lay heavy on the stomach, *eisbein*, pork shin slow-cooked in stock, (so-called because in Medieval times the bone would be subsequently used for ice-skates) *sauerkraut* and *bratkartoffeln*, pan-fried potatoes with garlic and onions.

At times it had seemed as if they were trying to incorporate every idea that came to them, fired by their desire to push the boundaries, when only two ideas were required. But along with many inspiring moments of insight and creativity there were also dreadful times of exhausted pessimism which descended on them like black, swollen rain clouds, the realisation that maybe they were not the architectural geniuses they had once considered themselves to be. Almost every decision entailed fierce arguments between the British and German architects until they all became burned out, physically and mentally shattered, sick of Berlin and its crazy pace. A prevailing sense grew in them that at Treptow they were dealing with a monster, which was now beyond their control.

CST did other competitions too but the focus throughout their time in Berlin was on the Treptow building. Ultimately what Mike feels he learned from the commission was the art of compromise—it was a lesson in Germanic pragmatism and British eccentricity. At the end of

OPPOSITE Treptow entrance elevation (top), and the subtly different rear elevation (bottom). The client only permitted limited areas of elaboration on corners and around entrances. Note the reference to the Goddard Laboratories by Louis Kahn.

ABOVE Mike Stiff and Hartmut Eichhorn (with unknown Siemens colleague) at a celebratory meal during the final months of the Treptow project.

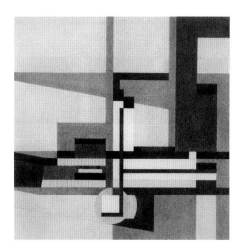

the project he was faced with an awkward decision to carry on with Doug Clelland his old tutor and mentor, or to go back to Trevillion and Blandy? Tired out from the unrelenting pace of the work in Berlin, sick of the commuting he had been doing for two years and sorely missing London, in the end it was not that difficult to decide where he would rather be. Andy also wanted his partner back on board, he and Richard Blandy had held things together admirably in Mike's absence but now they needed his input. On the personal side, due to his long, enforced absences (what he describes as his 'national service') family troubles had inevitably blown up and Mike was now fighting to save his marriage. He had no qualms about packing his bags and leaving Berlin for good.

AFTER BERLIN

By October 1994 the split with Doug Clelland was complete and Mike was back in London permanently. The UK economy was recovering and gathering momentum and London was once again the place to be. Creative energy was sizzling from the new digital industries sprouting up as the children of the dot com revolution began to engage their gaming skills to good effect.

In the wake of Treptow, CST looked at some Siemens work in the UK but the collaborative spark between them had gone out and they no longer had the appetite for working together. However, during the Berlin years, Mike had formed a solid friendship with Hartmut Eichhorn and Stiff + Trevillion later picked up a few residential commissions in Germany through him which they worked on from London. Andy had also maintained contact with Martin Stocks, Siemens' UK Development Manager since the Treptow era and they had looked at a couple of development sites for him in Hampshire and Dorset. A few months after the completion of their work in Berlin, Andy was contacted by Siemens UK regarding the possibility of a commission for them at Roke Manor, Romsey.

The partners were called for an interview. Their initial meeting was to be at the Siemen's UK headquarters in Sunley. Still trying to pay off their debts with the bank, neither Mike nor Andy owned a car at that time, so they took themselves and their weighty portfolio on the train from Waterloo Station down to Siemens HQ. On that first visit, so short of money they couldn't even afford a taxi, they had to walk the two miles from the station to Siemen's offices in the sweltering summer heat. They arrived sweating and a little embarrassed about their obvious circumstances—at that moment even the Bakelite Trabant from Mitte seemed like a luxurious memory of better times, the stable privileges of Communism contrasted with the pecuniary uncertainties of turbo-capitalism.

The prospective commission they discussed was for a research and innovation building which would incorporate an original nineteenth century manor house and its later additions, adding 6,000 square metres

of accommodation to the existing building, all in a lush, landscaped setting. Compared to the Jeremy Lloyd interview, everything was much more relaxed. Martin Stocks kindly drove them back to the station after lunch, rather admiring the austerity of their position—there was something utilitarian and austere, almost Germanic about it. By the time Mike and Andy arrived back in London at the end of a short train journey their PA already had the good news—they now had an exciting new commission.

Roke Manor Research was completed in 2002. During the 20 years since Wateringbury, Stiff + Trevillion had moved their architecture forward significantly, mainly as a direct result of the lessons Mike had learnt in Berlin working at the coalface. The intensity of Treptow, all that stress and deep thinking about theory and technology, discussions around on-site practices and learning about the logistics of running a large-scale project efficiently, had paid rich dividends. The partners now knew how to do big buildings and this new development would draw heavily on

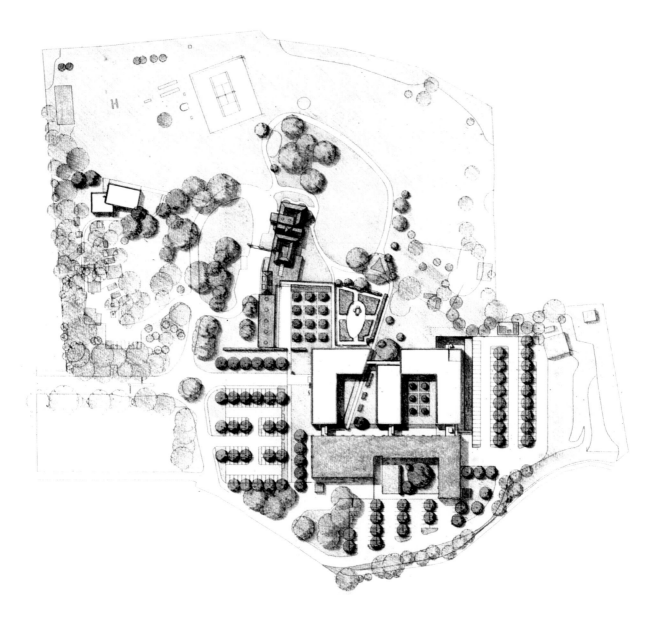

the Treptow experience but they hoped, with a new angle. It was to be strongly expressive of the Siemens ethos, geometric and spare, with a clearly articulated separation of the main architectural elements—frame, facade, glazing, roof and landscape. However it would also have a fresh, 'Stiff + Trevillion' feel to it—coherent, relaxed, client facing.

Unlike most of their previous commissions, which had focused on the interiors that in turn generated the external expression of the building, yielding little to the surrounding context, this was a building where the external spaces took over, dictating from outside to in, almost back to front. The new structures enclosed the landscape creating courtyards, which generated routes across the site, interweaving subtly into the geography of the building's interior. There were light references to the historical structures, for example the former eighteenth century walled garden was recognised in the courtyard pattern, a respectful nod back to the roots of their architectural thinking. It was, and remains, one of Stiff + Trevillion's most satisfying projects, emphasising the geometric order of the built form sitting within an Arcadian landscape.

Roke Manor Research
View from South East

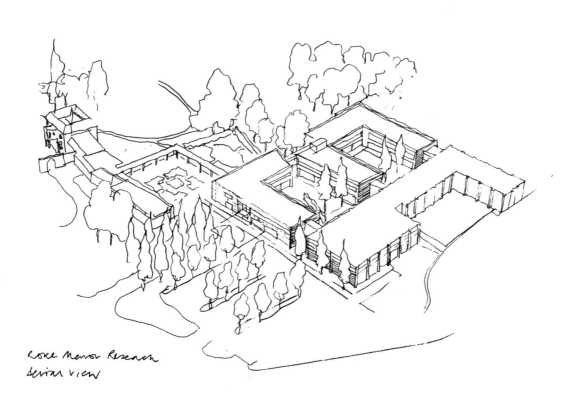

Roke Manor Research
Aerial view

114

ABOVE Roke Manor Research. The long wing was interrupted to accommodate an existing Horse Chestnut tree.

OPPOSITE TOP Roke Manor Research. View across the kitchen garden.

OPPOSITE BOTTOM Roke Manor Research, the dining room interior, with a large circular roof light edged in yellow to reflect warm light into the depths of the plan. A relaxing view of the courtyard garden is captured beyond, completed 1995.

The purely functional interiors contrasted with much of their previous work, it was a groundbreaking project for Stiff + Trevillion, a new European form of architecture which was all about context and content rather than image and impact. Roke Manor was to influence a lot of their new-build work over the following decade and was a first for the practice, the point where they really found their mojo. It was elegant, full of texture and clearly delineated colour, it appeared effortless in its delivery. It was also the first fully 'digital' project they had worked on. These were subtle differences but nevertheless significant ones. Rather than being overloaded with a plethora of ideas as with some of their earlier projects, Roke Manor had a clear sense of spatial hierarchy. The development is spare and rich at the same time; it has gravitas, a workplace in no-uncertain terms but also with a lightness of touch, which is in harmony with the landscaped setting and the rhythm of the working relationships within. It is harmonious, restful. The building's style eschews the mannerist posturing of their younger days in favour of an altogether more relaxed, collegiate spirit.

In 2000 Stiff + Trevillion secured another commission through the developer contact they had bumped into during their Christmas celebrations ten years earlier, Richard Draycott. Described by architectural writer Ellis Woodman in *Architecture Today* as "contemporary vernacular", Clarke House, is a speculative office building in Egham, a somewhat nondescript commuter-belt town in Surrey. The aim was to create a place which was both civic and full of character. Working with a limited palette of materials, red brick and concrete, and adopting a similar approach to that used at Roke Manor, they achieved a simple, expressive composition which manages to be both modern, like a simplified abstract painting playing with the traditional wall-to-window relationships, and also traditional, complex and rich, respectful of its semi-urban setting. It was a deft trick to pull off and one, which many young practices would find difficult, built on the hard won experience of the previous decade. Woodman describes the building as follows:

Where lesser architects would have treated the project as simple bread-and-butter work, Stiff + Trevillion have invested the project with real architectural ambition and produced a building of considerable refinement.... This Millennium year will see a string of spectacular Lottery-funded projects opening up and down the country. It is worth remembering that background buildings like Clarke House have a far greater role to play in determining the character of a town than any number of high profile architectural set pieces. Stiff + Trevillion's building exemplifies the level of care that such work demands.[7]

Both Roke Manor and Egham have transcendental qualities different from the ambitious but uncertain architectural grappling of their early work. These buildings are calm and mature, anticipating the more contemplative spirit of the new millennium, which was just around the corner. It was grown-up thinking—the architecture the partners were now producing was moving in the direction that they themselves wished to travel. Now in their mid-40s, their practice had turned the corner and they were secure but also wiser. Both men felt ready to embrace the next phase of practice.

NEW TECHNOLOGY

Writing in 1992, the architect Peter Eisenman (who was at that time building an architecturally influential apartment block in Berlin, adjacent to Checkpoint Charlie), stated that "since the Second World War a profound change had taken place in the way we interact with the world". He described this process as "the electronic paradigm", alluding to the shift from mechanical to electronic devices, which would come to increasingly dominate our lives by the end of the twentieth century.[8] In this category Eisenman included television, fax machines and photocopiers but what he did not predict was arguably the most profound transformation since the Industrial Revolution, the advent of the digital age and the widespread introduction of personal computers, mobile phones, the Internet and the World Wide Web.

Today, we know that even more significantly the electronic paradigm has revolutionised the way we communicate and access information and in particular has facilitated the birth of social media such as Facebook, Twitter, LinkedIn and numerous other interactive sites, which enable rapid social interaction amongst groups rather than just between individuals. If gamers and geeks were the first to latch on to the Internet to start making connections across the globe, the rest of us were not far behind. In the world of business the advertising industry recognised the potential of the vast audience they could reach through digital channels and quickly assumed innovative viral techniques. Soon global businesses were developing overnight through the power of online advertising alone.

Arguably every sector of our waking lives over the last 20 years has been affected by the all-pervading influence of computer technology and the

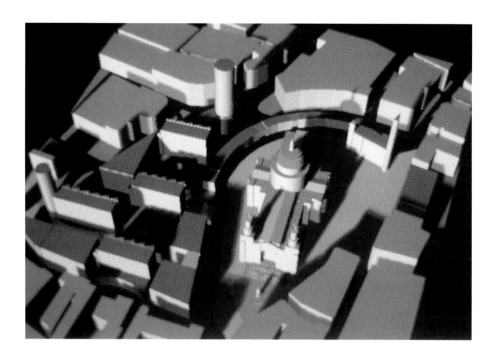

Internet—they simply cannot be ignored. From the late 1990s onwards they have been transforming and destroying business models across the board and nowhere has this been more profoundly felt than in the creative industries, such as graphic design and architecture.

When Mike Stiff had been working on the Treptow project in Berlin, most of the early design drawings had been produced in London in the studio. Mike recalls how last minute changes to drawings were almost impossible, since in the days before Computer Aided Design (CAD), everything was painstakingly drawn in ink on tracing paper. When amendments were required, unbelievably a razor blade, held at 45 degrees to the surface of the paper, had to be carefully manipulated to scratch out any unwanted lines. The aim was to remove the top surface layer of paper in order to make the correction without gouging a hole all the way through—it required the manual dexterity of a brain surgeon.

Mike and Andy were 'digital immigrants' not 'digital natives', with their experience of studying and training in the pre-digital age seeming quaint and old-fashioned to architecture students of today. It entailed long, arduous hours working on hand-drawn renderings, sometimes with carefully graded shadows to give depth and texture (Sciagraphy— the science of shadows—was a subject still taught in their first year at architecture school), sometimes using Letraset sheets of tone which had to be peeled off their backing paper, stuck onto the previously unrendered drawing and cut to fit the appropriate shape with a scalpel. Geometrically constructed perspectives were made using long pieces of string to generate accurate converging and diverging planes. The processes they were obliged to use were largely manual and the tools at their disposal antiquated— even the photocopier was still in its infancy during their time at the polytechnic and only came into widespread use towards the tail end of their studies—although the training they received was rigorous and the skills it fostered invaluable.

Around the time the fees started to come in from the Treptow project the partners decided to make their first venture into digitally generated CAD. During the Berlin project, drawings from the practice had been plotted in the studio in London, printed out and then sent by courier in time for the site meetings in Germany the next morning. They were even delivered by hand if time was tight. As Mike recalls, "in those days it took an hour to plot an A0 drawing, we would spend all night printing the floor plans and race to Heathrow on the tube to get the first plane to Berlin". It was in short an archaic, painstaking, time-consuming process.

In January 1992 the practice acquired three brand new Apple Macs—big, grey, lumpy, lozenge-shaped boxes, streets away from the slimline, minimalist elegance of today's Apple hardware. For a small, struggling business like theirs this new technology was expensive, only just on the edge of being financially viable. However, the simple, rapid efficiency of digital drawings, compared to their time-hungry, hand-drawn renderings convinced the partners that going digital was a commercial imperative. Evolve or die was the maxim and they appreciated that the investment in new technologies was not only going to be about switching to CAD. This was the dawning of a new age of endless possibilities and an online presence was becoming essential for any commercial practice that was to compete effectively. Within a few years social networking would become an essential tool for marketing architectural services and for mainstream commercial practices like Stiff + Trevillion it was now vital to up their game and make sure they were visible and accessible through a variety of channels. The two partners realised they would have to learn a lot of new tricks.

However, Mike and Andy themselves had very little time to spare. They were working flat-out and could not take time out to return to college for formal CAD training. It would have to be a case of learning what they could on the job, and eventually, getting the right people in, to guide them through the labyrinthine possibilities and arrive at the best solutions.

In this respect, Andy Stiff, Mike's brother, significantly aided them. A fine artist who trained at the Chelsea School of Art and something of a pioneer within the creative world of digital media, he became an important channel of knowledge-transfer for the practice during those early years. In his gently understated way, Andy Stiff cajoled the partners into further and continuous investment in technologies, for example producing the first in-house perspectives for presentation to clients. Most importantly he was able to show them that the digital revolution was worth the investment of time and personnel as well as hard cash because the potential rewards were legion. He began to explore the wider capabilities the new systems implied across areas such as marketing and graphic design in order to promote a different sort of business profile. He unpacked a whole plethora of new possibilities regarding image building for the practice, through an ever-evolving, dynamic website and savvy use of emerging social networking channels. Production and construction processes soon became much more streamlined too and the practice developed an efficient document storage and retrieval system to gradually replace the traditional stacks of paper-filled folders and portfolios.

Good design and word-of-mouth recommendations were no longer enough to let Stiff + Trevillion prosper in the digital age. In order to grow the practice had to change, embrace modernity and be geared up to address a wider global audience. Their business was not just about an end product now, a building, or a set of architectural theories, they needed to develop a more coherent ethos. They needed to focus not just on the individual client (although this was still an important relationship), but on the group of partners, directors and employees who were Stiff + Trevillion, and the collaborative kind of fellowship which was evolving within the practice in place of the 'us and them' mentality of the old workplace mores.

It's important to appreciate that during this era, although Andy Stiff was ahead of the game, there was still a great deal of uncertainty around their use of software in planning and designing projects, no one was totally sure what the right technology was for the jobs in hand, or how they should adapt their working practices as a result. On complex projects, how could they ensure that their systems were compatible with the structural engineer's drawn information for example? Was the contractor's technology on the same level as their own? These considerations had implications on costs and on scheduling and required being adequately thought through. Production tasks like developing perspectives and amending drawings now became easier and communication between designers and contractors was enormously improved by the advent of email and mobile phones, which undoubtedly increased profits on many jobs. On the negative side however, the cost of upgrading software and hardware every other year was significant and had to be factored into increased fees. Most importantly for Mike as the chief designer, what effect did CAD have on their traditional approach to conceptualising buildings? In creative terms, how was the new technology going to be made to work for them? How much of the design work does CAD actually aid? And crucially, would it change the architecture itself?

Mike and Andy are the only two people now working at Stiff + Trevillion who do not know how to draw digitally, who do not use SketchUp to generate outline perspectives, who do not know CAD. Why is this? The answer may partly be that they felt a certain resistance to digital technology, a need to keep their distance from it, to control rather than to be controlled by such a powerful unknown quantity. It is also partly to do with perception. Undoubtedly both Mike and Andy believe in the primacy of the pencil. It may be a generational thing but it is how they were taught and it is how they think, express their ideas. Put simply, to translate your conceptual thinking into a quick annotated perspectival sketch is still a fundamentally important skill. It is one of those alchemical skills which most clients find very appealing and impressive, it sets the architect apart as a creative, as an artist. As he talks, he thinks, he draws.

It has an immediacy, which takes representation beyond the surface and gives expression to a deeper, more rounded interpretation of the architectural idea, a process which goes far beyond 'talkitecture'.

What is perplexing to both Mike and Andy is the idea that many young architects who come to work in their office nowadays only know how to draw in CAD or SketchUp. Except for a few schools of architecture, for example the University of Liverpool which doesn't permit students to use computers until second year, the pencil skill is not taught anymore. Few schools insist on students learning to draw by hand with a T-square and pencil, or make physical models in cardboard or wood. Now there are even 3-D model-making machines which will carve-out the form from a plastic block for you, a million miles from feeling and forming it yourself, a physical experience which can be traced back to the first finger-painted art found in cave paintings. As the great twentieth century American architect Frank Lloyd Wright asserted in relation to the use of his wooden Froebel blocks in kindergarten, through handling those warm maple wood forms and physically forming shapes, with the immediacy of brain to hand, an essential lifelong understanding was established, "through this, form follows feeling", he stated.[9]

Today, Stiff believes there is a certain type of "digital architecture" which is too easy and encourages laziness, if placed in the wrong hands. It becomes a sort of extruded form of shape-making, which simply does not reflect the complex humanistic values he knows his clients expect in Stiff + Trevillion's architecture. You can't design someone's home on a computer. When Mike sketches quickly to show his assistant architect the qualities he is looking for within an imagined three-dimensional space, as he has for 30 years, does the CAD-schooled neo-graduate understand where he is coming from? What is the dynamic for those who do not draw in the old-fashioned way? The ethos of the practice as conceived by the partners, must be able to percolate down through the team by way of a common language, both verbal and visual, equipping all the colleagues with the set of common ethical notions, which defines the work and produces excellent building design that stands the test of time.

EDIBLE ARCHITECTURE

In architecture there are some types of work, such as restaurant design, shop refurbishment and interiors generally, which has a limited shelf life. If you are the type of architect who details everything, owns the project and almost resents the owners hanging a picture on the wall, this can prove difficult to accept—the amount of work and thought put into the project can end up feeling disproportionate to the essentially ephemeral end result achieved. Since the 1980s, whilst other more established practices eschewed interior design as somehow being beneath them, Stiff + Trevillion had taken on this sort of work with enthusiasm, understanding that though the flavour is different, there is satisfaction to be gained from getting it right; also that this sort of work can be very

Nighthawks,
Edward Hopper,
1942, oil on canvas,
84.1 x 152.4 cm

lucrative. The design of bars and restaurants, their social interface, their atmosphere and detail, the effect of all these architectural themes on their clientele, have since the earliest days been a passionate interest.

It's October 2013 and I'm sitting in the refurbished Costa Coffee at the end of Great Portland Street close to Oxford Circus, one of Stiff + Trevillion's recent commissions. This is an L-shaped space on a street corner. Full-height glazing turns the corner and from the outside the facade has the transparency of that iconic Edward Hopper painting *Nighthawks*. However, unlike the melancholy emptiness of that city image, this interior is vibrant and welcoming. I have my back to one of the end walls semi-reclining as I write on a soft velour bench seat, comforting during my Monday morning first-coffee-of-the-day rush. Behind me a large abstract mural of what might be lilies enlivens the wall, patterned in three drenched colours, pink, lemon and amber on a salmon-brown background. It softens, adds a hint of the natural world to a space, which is for the most-part wholly functional, striving to simply sell as many highly priced coffees a day as is feasible.

In front of me the well-proportioned almost double-height room is illuminated by a range of diverse pendant light fittings, drooping down in neat rows like droplets. They help to organise the tables beneath them, providing intimacy and gentle task lighting fit for writing or conversing. The cafe is full of similar modish, well-practiced tropes, yet it feels authentic. It works both on the functional level and stylistically as a derivation of the best that Rome, Havana or New York has to offer. It also encapsulates that distinctive Stiff + Trevillion spatial modulation—modernism mixed with heritage chic.

Exposed air-ducts and cable trays create visual orderliness across the irregularly exposed ceiling planes above. However, the principal is to retain the messy patina of age as much as possible within the frame of a clear corporate image, work with it rather than cover it over, allow the eye to take curious pleasure from the memory of what previous uses the isolated surfaces now suggest. Some of the original floor finishes are apparent, the shiny wood block flooring, circa 1961, has been retained in the short arm of the L, bare London stock brickwork can be seen starkly exposed in various areas of the room, contrasting with the polished smoothness of adjacent olive and puce coloured plaster wall panels. To my left there is a bleached cladding panel in raw, distressed ash, which runs around two sides of the space modulating the service desk. Aged wood transmogrifies into polished black granite. Reflective black and white wall tiles, aluminium work surfaces and high-level glazed screens bisect each other creating subsidiary spatial tonality. The iconic Gaggia coffee machine is at the centre of everything like an old-fashioned steam engine, puffing and spluttering noisily. It is the focus of the space, that and the Roman sink with its constantly flowing fountain-like tap. It's a busy space but also one which is calm and comforting. There is a resonant buzz of conversation that is never too loud. The acoustics are perfect. It is London yet it has the tantalising air of somewhere else, a mixture of New York West Side and Rome's Piazza Navona. Clearly it is designed with the confidence, which comes from years of experience.

This is Stiff + Trevillion's new prototype city hang-out and, due to its incredible commercial success—coffee sales increased from 10,000 per week to 15,000 immediately after their redesign—it was the first of many similarly designed spaces for the Whitbread-owned Costa chain. It illustrates perfectly what good design can do for the bottom line. Cafe and restaurant design is now one of Stiff + Trevillion's core disciplines and their touch is assured.

Reflecting on this type of cafe culture environment, now quite commonplace in Britain, it's perhaps worth recalling what the typical UK drinking and eating experience was like in the 1970s and 1980s in Britain. Firstly it was almost impossible to get a cup of fresh coffee. There was a famous advertising campaign during the 1980s, which appeared on television featuring the sound of a loud coffee machine gurgling and spluttering in the kitchen of a rich, smooth bachelor's apartment. The camera then glides from the living room where the glamorous girl is waiting, to the kitchen to reveal that there is no coffee machine at all. Instead the bachelor is mixing a cup of powdered Nescafe by hand, all the while making the whooshing sounds of the nonexistent coffee maker. The message was clear—even the sophisticated among us don't bother with fresh coffee when they can get it readymade from a jar. It was called "instant coffee" and in Britain it was what most people drank, essentially a coffee-flavoured drink.

Trying to buy a healthy, decently priced lunch then was equally challenging. The typical working day office lunch was in a pub and

consisted of an anaemic sausage roll washed down with a pint of Double Diamond. A bottled tomato juice with Worcester Sauce was considered the height of suburban refinement as an aperitif. Garlic was something for vampires, which the British never ate because it was smelly foreign stuff. Even the dubious pleasures of McDonalds did not then exist in the UK—fast food, as we know it today, was yet to arrive on these shores.

Similarly, affordable restaurants where people could eat out on a special occasion were limited to chains like the ubiquitous Berni Inn, usually a sub-prime pub serving sub-prime steaks, and the so-called "*trattoria*", all kitsch rusticity evoking a nostalgic image of rural Italy between the wars. In those far off times before global transportation made fresh food available and imported ingredients were difficult to come by, there was a heavy reliance on pasta and tomato sauce. Since immigrant restaurateurs cynically maintained that the English would eat anything and had little culinary sophistication, there had been little motivation to make more of an effort. Then there were the newly emerging Indian eateries, all flock wallpaper, grubby floral carpets and cheap ingredients disguised with strong chili and eccentric colouring. The staple was hot-as-hell curry best eaten when you were slightly inebriated, the perfect Saturday night meal for British blokes in that sloppy era.

Stiff's first restaurant memory is of his father taking him to the original Pizza Express in London's Museum Street around 1970. This was then a one-off place, a former dairy which had received a light makeover and been efficiently converted to serve that then unknown Neapolitan staple,

PREVIOUS PAGES Costa Coffee Farringdon, with raw painted breezeblock and glazed ceramic tiles creating a smoothly textured finish, 2010.

ABOVE Costa Coffee, Great Portland Street—a new conceptual identity, which significantly improved the brand's effectiveness, 2010.

OPPOSITE Costa Coffee, Great Portland Street—lounge area, meeting point with glazed screening to provide a sense of enclosure.

the pizza. This was *cucina povera* using relatively cheap ingredients—fresh mozzarella cheese, homemade tomato sauce and fresh herbs on a base of flat bread prepared on the premises with ingredients, which had actually been imported from Italy. The pizzas were served straight from the traditional wood oven by two chefs dressed as Venetian gondoliers who retrieved them on long wooden shovels.

That simple, well-prepared dinner, served in a pared back but evocative setting, was in many ways a defining moment for the young Stiff. He noticed that the food didn't come from a dingy kitchen hidden away somewhere at the back of the premises, the open pizza oven had been configured as a key feature and was central to the layout—in full public view so that diners could see the fresh ingredients being used. This design seemed to lend a perfect authenticity to the room, it resonated with a feeling of hearth and home yet retained the quality of a public space. Somehow it felt healthier, more authentic, reassuring, the fact that you could actually see the food being prepared. He looked around and noticed how the exposed ceilings and original arches of the former dairy had

Pizza Express, Herne Hill, south-east London, Stiff + Trevillion went back to the brand's original Enzo Apicella-style graphics, creating a stunning one-off design, 2010.

provided a perfect frame for the conversion. Most of the original features had been retained and the high, vaulted ceilings were simply covered with a veneer of white wall tiles in a light, clean refurbishment, which retained the spirit of the place. There was definitely an element of historicism but the overall effect was modern, simple—no fake Italian rusticity here.

Pizza Express was probably the first branded restaurant chain in the UK worth its salt. Its ethos is still based on a limited combination of simple ingredients, fast efficient service and spare spatial treatment that provides a modern, functional setting for a convivial family eating experience. This has proved a winning combination as a design template for the 400 plus Pizza Express restaurants which have mushroomed in the ensuing years. You might call it "edible architecture"—the space as a perfect match to the food and drink on offer. This complementarity of food and setting was to form a benchmark in Mike's imagination for one of his first restaurant commissions, Alan Yau's, wagamama in central London

After the exhilarating student experience of Rome the partners went on to explore other cities—Berlin, Munich, Milan, New York, Boston, Havana, even Tokyo—making research trips a part of their lifestyle. Holidays were for the best part of 20 years, rarely spent sitting on a beach; rather their family leisure time was largely spent broadening their aesthetic and cultural horizons.

Visiting bars and restaurants was also an essential part of their social existence, part of their idea of a vibrant public life played out in the city. This came from the European tradition they had imbibed during their education and Mike Stiff in particular was constantly curious, not just about the overall architectural tone of a particular bar, restaurant or shop, but also about noting the particular details, which contributed to the ambience—the features you could see, hear and touch, enhancing the whole experience. For example, in Rome he loved the way in which running water was an imminent presence in the city, not just in the streets and squares outside but also inside, with a mini-fountain or a constantly flowing tap just in view over the bar top, investing the room with a vital element, refreshing the eye, a visual focus for cool reflection away from the hot midday sun. In the city of fountains it has a symbolic, as well as sensory, dimension.

130

According to Mike Stiff, this type of critical observation is an important skill within an architect's knowledge base, which can all too often be excessively theoretical and subjective, focused on trends and the latest article in *Homes and Gardens* rather than on any hard and fast evidence as to what works and has long-term value.[10] A client will say, "I like this" or "I don't like that" on a whim, without any good reason or deep understanding of its value and inexperienced architects are often too swayed by this. For a serious discipline, architecture is too often susceptible to the vagaries of changing fashion. Stiff believes that the skill a budding architect really needs to acquire is this "learning to see", that ability to critically observe and record an architectural response to a given environment. On every trip that he makes Mike has a small notebook at the ready for recording, filing, filling his "memory attic" with a catalogue of his direct experiences of public spaces, bars, restaurants, galleries, museums. From this eclectic collection of impressions and observations Stiff's knowledge has grown and grown. It is a form of constant documentation which has become second nature to him and the resultant rich bank of evidence-based research is in constant use within the practice as a vital reference point in discussions with clients or when conceptualising a new interior with colleagues.

To young architects in the practice he will always explain his ideas by way of a building or an interior he knows, describing and illustrating his experience of it and encouraging his assistants to get out there and visit it, feel it, just as his tutors urged him to do when he was at college. It may seem time-consuming and self-indulgent to some in today's frenetic world

of Internet-based information overload but Mike firmly believes your own senses and responses are the best critical filters. This in many ways is how the wagamama commission came about.

Stiff + Trevillion's first major restaurant commission came through graphic designer Patrick Roberts, an old friend who introduced them to Alan Yau, the owner of a couple of lucrative Chinese takeaways in Peterborough. It was to be a difficult experience but one, which was critical in the evolving story of their practice.

Alan Yau had travelled to Japan in the late 1980s and was consumed by a simple idea, the noodle bar, a ubiquitous feature of Japanese cities but a then unknown concept in London. Alan Yau was a young entrepreneur whose parents left Hong Kong for King's Lynn in the 1970s. He was determined to bring this eating concept to the West and believed that the still fragile economy of London was ready for something new. The concept was simple, a noodle bar in the Japanese tradition but designed as a sit-down, snack-style restaurant. It would be minimalist in style but warm and inviting, a destination where customers would be encouraged to come in, sit down, eat and enjoy but not to dwell for too long— essentially a more evolved fast food outlet with Eastern panache. In terms of layout he envisaged fixed elongated shared bench tables and bench seating, functional rather than comfortable but creating a social eating experience. The menu would be reasonably priced, focused mainly on

Presentation drawing exhibited at the Royal Academy. 90 degree abstracted axonometric in pencil and crayon by Mike Stiff, illustrating the first and original wagamama restaurant, Bloomsbury, in the heart of London's Museum quarter, 1993.

Interior view of wagamama with,
on the left, the servery and the
semi-open kitchen, an innovative
arrangement for a London
restaurant at that time, 1993.

ramen noodles and generally promoting the benefits of the Japanese
diet with green tea and other wholesome Asian staples available. Most
importantly, it would have an open kitchen running across the back of
a single canteen-type space.

Courageously, Yau put all of his capital on the line in order to take the
project forward. He quickly found suitable premises, securing a lease on
a basement space located in a Bloomsbury backstreet close to the British
Museum. It was central but without the West End rental prices, it was to
be one of the first lifestyle restaurants in the capital.

Initially, Yau hired John Pawson to come up with a scheme and to develop
the concept. A pioneering "minimalist", Pawson had become reasonably
well-known as the architect who only allowed 100 books into his home
due to his strict rules on purity and tidiness of the spaces he had designed
for his family. At the time, this seemed like a rather eccentric idea. Now
perhaps, in an era when more and more of us are forced to live in smaller
and smaller spaces and storage is a constant issue, it makes greater sense.
Pawson was well connected and astute, fashionable and particularly adept

when it came to generating free publicity. To Yau, he seemed like the right man for the job.

However in Pawson, Alan Yau had unwittingly commissioned a designer who was to prove extremely uncompromising in his own architectural vision. He insisted on the use of top-grade materials, expensively designed and purpose-made fixtures and fittings, which could transform the lightless basement into the sort of empty white minimalist space that was perfect for an art gallery, or for stylish, empty photographs in an architectural tome, but perhaps not so appropriate for a busy central London fast food restaurant. Most critically Pawson's monochrome minimalist vision was not going to come cheap.

For this elegant design, which required the use of 50 mm thick white Carrara marble table tops and lots of etched glass, the construction costs came in at over £500,000—three times the available budget—and at this point the viability of the scheme was beginning to unravel. This was intended to be a £10 per head canteen, rather than a £50 per head restaurant experience. Naturally the restauranteur and his family were getting jittery—the recession wasn't over yet and the set-up figures for the business now looked terrifying.

Cut your losses, pay-off the consultants and retreat his backers advised. Yau was demoralised and on the point of abandoning the project when Patrick Roberts suggested they source a second more modest design, through his friends Stiff + Trevillion. Up until that time, Mike and Andy had actually worked on very few of these sorts of commissions, however on meeting them, Yau felt he could trust them and decided to give it a go—his last throw of the dice on the problematic project.

Sensing that the noodle bar idea might be a winning formula, Roberts had managed to persuade Mike that together they could try to save the project by designing a more basic scheme using low-cost, stripped back natural materials wherever possible. There would probably be no fee if it failed, however the longer they thought about it the more Patrick and Mike warmed to the idea. It was all-new for London and therefore a risk but on the other hand it was a tried-and-tested formula transplanted from another part of the world where it was commercially successful. Why should something that was a cultural phenomenon in the East not catch on in the West? This put a different perspective on things and Stiff + Trevillion instinctively felt that the moment was right and the restaurant would be a hit. Besides, Mike found the whole Japanese influence intriguing.

The problem of costs was central to the commission; the need for a more streamlined construction process than was normal. Stiff + Trevillion have always been very engaged by the relationship between the intellectual flow of ideas and their physical translation into real architecture. The point for them is not just to talk and draw without any end-product, their motivation is almost always about building, seeing things come

together on-site, watching the scheme come out of the ground, or observing their work on an interior transforming an existing space into something wholly new.

As the culmination of a long creative process, the eventual translation of the drawn form into the built form, seeing their building physically rise to completion, has an almost erotic appeal for many architects. The transformational esoteric precept of idea-form-matter is nowhere so apparent as in the discipline of architecture and for most professionals in the field actually realising a bricks-and-mortar building is the payback for all the other problems that are part of the process. Stiff + Trevillion are no exceptions—walking through and around a completed project, seeing it, warts and all, in three dimensions, is always the best payback.

Realising the noodle bar project within the confines of the available budget, compromising without losing the spatial quality, was where the architects' skill was going to be really tested in this case. Mike and Richard Blandy went to work with some relish but soon found

The Bloomsbury wagamama full of people sharing communal tables during the first hectic months after its opening.

that cutting the costs on the Pawson scheme was going to be almost impossible. Stiff + Trevillion therefore decided on a redesign in the spirit of Pawson's original vision but using different materials which would subtly change it. Chestnut was proposed for the floors with the bench tables in ash, substituting the marble and other expensive finishes originally proposed and replacing glitz with a cool, stripped-back, natural feel. Vinyl was introduced in some unseen areas to reduce the overall costs and improve functionality and they designed their own lighting scheme rather than commissioning specialist consultants. They even undertook the outline services schedules themselves, producing their own performance specifications in order to minimise the upfront cost of specialist expertise.

The new scheme had other advantages apart from saving money. It was warm where Pawson's scheme had been cold, the natural materials and the selective use of colour gave it a more welcoming, easy informality appropriate to the vibe Yau hoped to create. It was still recognisably 'Eastern' in style but possessed a greater sense of appropriacy—the pared-back simplicity of the East melded with the functionality of the West, rather than an empty architectural rhetoric in all of its pristine perfection. It had evolved into a different, more relevant concept and in addition the planning and functionality was now spot-on, with aspects such as the subsidiary spaces for coats, WCs and product storage all in exactly the right places.

Having approved the scheme, the client then asked them to bear down on costs further—he was concerned that it might all go wrong when the contractors started on-site and started racking up the dreaded 'extras'. The good working relations the practice had cultivated over a number of previous residential projects with the main contractors were especially valuable now. Richard Blandy reassured Yau by sourcing a specialist shop-fitting contractor through their network who was willing to work to a fixed price, adopting a sort of design and build approach appropriate for the later stages of a recession. At last, Alan gave them the green light to go ahead and start. The new restaurant opened in 1992 and was christened "wagamama" after the Japanese expression for "a selfish, rebellious child". It also has the connotation of a person being demanding, an idea enshrined in the expectations of the typical wagamama customer.

Alan Yau was undoubtedly a visionary, a vaguely mystical and principled man, very much a synthesis of Eastern mystique and Western pragmatism. Famously he carried no credit cards, didn't smoke or drink, had no agenda to promote other than the success of the business venture he was promoting. He was fastidious in the detail, a natural entrepreneur. Yau now hired Japanese chefs and waiters, which helped to give the place authenticity. The London restaurant market, which had been devastated by the recession, could hardly believe wagamama's overnight success. Noodles for goodness sake?! Who wants that kind of food, the critics screamed? Like Pizza Express 25 years previously, this was taking basic ingredients eaten by poor people in a distant land and making them a bit special, investing them with the glamour of the exotic in a super-cool environment which was predicated on the architecture.

To the public it seemed innovative and stylish and the message soon spread by word of mouth. At the end of the first month, the 105 seat restaurant was serving 1,500 people a day, at a time when similar establishments of that size might expect 300 customers at most. At an average of £10 per meal, daily turnover was soon about £15,000, an almost unheard-of sum for a fast food outlet. For the first few years, wagamama was so successful that there were queues running round the corner all day long and into the night. Booking was not permitted in the best fast food tradition, but for the young Londoners standing in-line during those early days it seemed like the fashionable place to be. wagamama had become an overnight sensation.

Alan Yau's reputation was made. Although over the next 25 years many others jumped on the bandwagon of Japanese cuisine in its various guises until London was awash with Asian noodle and sushi bars as the natural, healthy, low-fat alternative to burgers and pizzas, he was the one who had got there first.

The press were soon on the case. wagamama's runaway success was an engaging story—the radical new restaurant experience—and the concept was viewed as being ahead of the curve. It was also interpreted as a bellwether event, a prediction of better days ahead and an indicator that the recession was on the way out. However, things got a little complicated as, in time honoured tradition, one of the journalists reporting on the story failed to check her facts properly, and reported that Pawson was the author of the stylish interior.

Fay Maschler, the journalist in question, was an influential restaurant critic at the *Evening Standard*. Dining at wagamama with Pawson and Yau, she was struck by the minimalist interior with its clever Japanese feel, combined with the tasty unusual food and the service systems, which worked like a dream, discreet yet efficient. It all had a natural, upbeat rhythm in which the fast turnaround of the orders never felt rude—this was one of the things that made wagamama Mark 1 so popular and ultimately lucrative. She was also very impressed by what she thought was Pawson's fine work on the design. She concluded in her article that this was a unique new eating experience, where the vibe of the East was represented through a finely-tuned Western architectural space. The next day her glowing restaurant review appeared in London's paper. It was, she said, "the most exciting development this year in eating out". Everyone was name-checked, including the "ground-breaking interior design" by John Pawson. Stiff + Trevillion were not mentioned at all.

Stiff + Trevillion protested but Alan Yau was largely oblivious, more interested in getting a good review for the food than in discussing the finer points of the restaurant's interior architecture. Over the next few weeks an unholy row broke out with legal letters flying to and fro between the two practices, articles in the press and a simmering sense of injustice at the offices of Stiff + Trevillion.

In the end John Pawson withdrew any claim to the finished design in a hand-written letter to Mike. However, Stiff + Trevillion had to accept that Pawson had conceived it but crucially had not designed it. Despite Pawson's hasty retraction, from a publicity perspective it was too late, the story had run. Stiff + Trevillion merely seemed like executive architects, with the new 'minimalism' being attributed to the other better-known designer. A significant PR opportunity had been missed.

Hard lessons were learned from the experience however. The fact was that the partners had known about Pawson's original design when they had agreed to step in and Mike and Andy both realised that had they sought and received written confirmation at the outset that they were to be cited as the sole authors for a new scheme, all of this unpleasantness could have been avoided. They had been too busy sorting out other things but this was a critical piece of micro-management, which had gone astray.

They both realised that they had not thought ahead properly and consequently had missed the opportunity to milk the success of wagamama. In architecture, securing the next job is often based on what potential clients know about the previous one, particularly when a practice is trying to establish itself in a new specialist area of design, and they had neglected to capitalise on this. It was a salutary lesson and brought home the realisation that they knew absolutely nothing about PR and how to play the media. This would have to change.

RESTAURANTS BECOME A SPECIALIST AREA

The story of wagamama had already done the rounds and any possible benefit in terms of publicity had been lost. However, there were a couple of moves they could still make in an attempt to redress the balance, the first based on well-judged pragmatism, the second an emotionally-charged reaction to the huge sense of injustice still felt by Mike.

Firstly, sharing the cost with Roberts, they had the space photographed professionally. Some text and a couple of conceptual drawings were added and the photographer turned the piece into a neat A4 size brochure, expensively printed on glossy card. This they sent out to all of the main journals and newspapers and furthermore to 1,500 potential clients. Despite the exercise costing almost as much as their entire fee for the job, it did prove to be a smart move. The restaurant mogul Garry Hawkes of caterers Gardner Merchant picked it up and they were called in to consult on, and eventually were commissioned to design, City Rhodes for TV chef Gary Rhodes and his financial backers.

Stiff + Trevillion articulated the extremely low first floor dining space in a strikingly sculptural manner, with the ceiling curving around the junctions

between the horizontal and the vertical of the walls. With its sophisticated lighting system, the effect was to make the whole appear to float above the diners' heads, a sensation which was further enhanced by the mirrors above the banquette, angled to further blur the boundaries of the space. This trick has evolved to become a trademark Stiff + Trevillion motif, enabling the focus of the diner's sight to rest and relax on distant horizons rather than to be intensively fixed full-time on their partner's gaze across the table. With its subtle spatial dialogue between the lightness of their interventions and the heaviness of the existing Brutalist building within which they had to work, it was tantalising and subtle, corporate 'R&R' at its best.

The scheme was a big success both in terms of its execution and the prestige it generated in that well-heeled part of London, the expanding financial quarter. Like seeds planted in the most fertile part of the flood plain, its fame bloomed overnight and the restaurant garnered rave reviews. The architects' reputation flourished as City Rhodes became a well-loved, almost iconic place to eat for the city expense account brigade.

City Rhodes was completed in 1998 and became a suitable riposte to the authorship confusion over wagamama. Alan Yau made amends by introducing the practice to the Royal China Group, specialists in a more upmarket brand of Asian cuisine, and Stiff + Trevillion subsequently went on to design the influential Satsuma Restaurant in Wardour Street in 1998, again with great success for both the practice and for the client.

The Satsuma commission coincided with some exhibition design work the practice was undertaking for the Royal Academy. Peter Murray had introduced Mike to Maryanne Stevens who had a keen interest in promoting architecture through the RA. Stiff + Trevillion had been asked to design an exhibition that reviewed the work of British architects as the century drew to a close. Called New Urban Environments, it had its debut in Tokyo and went on to Hiroshima, Guangzhou, Beijing and Hong Kong. As it was a large and complex exhibition the architects needed to set up each stage of the show. At the same time Mike was asked to collaborate with Tadao Ando's office in Osaka on an exhibition of his work to be held at the RA in London. Visiting these and other Far Eastern cities was to prove invaluable to the Stiff + Trevillion memory bank.

Both Mike and Andy went to set up the Tokyo leg, and took the opportunity to explore the city, catch up with friends who were working there and to visit an old friend of Sara Trevillion's in a small, snowy traditional town called Takayama. The visit was pivotal in many ways, not least because Mike and Andy were encouraged to drink "lucky water" from a sacred spring in one of the temples they visited. To this day the usually pragmatic pair still believe that this was the moment when the fortunes of the practice changed.

Seeing traditional Japanese architecture in its natural environment really informed the Satsuma project. The use of rough timber shuttered concrete, was contrasted with the same timber on the walls. wagamama style tables and benches were used and the terrazzo floor with white stones in a black matrix made reference to the temple gardens in Kyoto. It also led to a series of drawings that was to form the basis for a solo exhibition of Mike's work in 1996. It was a memorable trip.

139

Satsuma was an important moment in the development of the restaurant sector for the practice. It banished the wagamama incident to the archives, and developed that white minimalism into a warmer more crafted interior architecture that:

creates a contemplative character to the interior space without lapsing into austerity or pretentiousness. In a curious way the detailing, materials and Scandinavian and Japanese influences echoes the late-1950s. At the same time the influence of Le Corbusier is ever present in the architects' choice of colours and their spatial concerns. (Russell Brown, *Architecture Today,* Issue 91.)

Similar restaurant commissions continued through to the end of the decade, all of them original and distinctive, respectful of the client's ideas, each interior designed as a one-off project. By the beginning of the noughties the practice had gained quite a reputation for its skill in addressing the needs of numerous one-off restaurant, cafe and bar owners wishing to move their brand forward. It seemed this sort of architecture—the interior-scape—was finally being viewed as a necessity rather than as an expensive luxury.

OPPOSITE City Rhodes restaurant, London, 1998. Note the low-level horizontal mirrors behind the tables—a Stiff + Trevillion motif—and on the left-side wall, Victor Pasmore lithographs.

TOP Ando exhibition at the Royal Academy, 1998.

BOTTOM New urban environments: a travelling Royal Academy exhibition in Japan and China, 1998–2000.

Takayama   michaelstiff.

ABOVE Drawing by Mike Stiff of one of the traditional timber framed houses in Takayama (Gifu Prefecture). Takayama is known for its fine carpentry.

OPPOSITE Satsuma Restaurant, Wardour Street, showing the rough boarded shuttered concrete used in the main dining space, a technique they had initially seen at the National Theatre.

Something of a boom in the whole industry then ensued, fuelled by the enormous popularity of celebrity TV chefs such as Gordon Ramsey, Jamie Oliver and Anton Mossiman. Significantly, they often presented their TV cookery shows outdoors in exotic locations—Tuscany, the Dordogne, Istanbul—which in a sense illustrated how important the drama of the event and the architecture of the food's setting had become. Cooking was no longer something which happened in a hidden room at the back of the house, it had acquired an element of theatre. Part of the pleasure of eating was now firmly bound up with its context and culture, all of the senses were engaged in its appreciation.

As the economy improved, Stiff + Trevillion were now perfectly positioned to take advantage of these booming times. Not only were they designing high-spec, one-off projects for clients wishing to optimise the culinary experience at the top-end of the market, they were increasingly engaged with mid-range high street chains too, brands like the family-friendly Giraffe and Le Pain Quotidian, the archetypal French-themed eatery, which were now becoming a staple of well-heeled highstreets up and down the country.

Since 2007, the practice has designed a sequence of Jamie's Italian restaurants, designed as a one-off, although with some similarities in

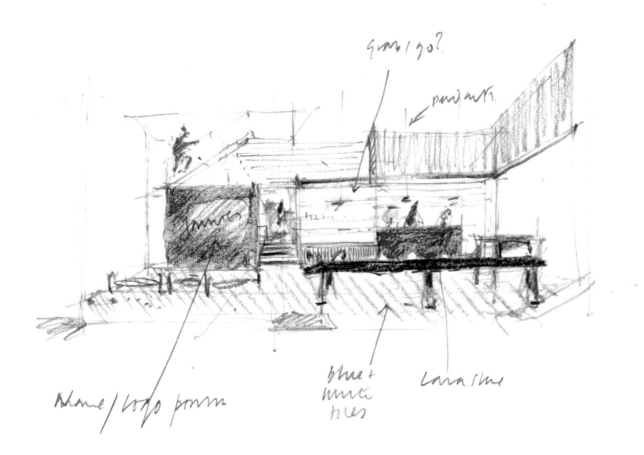

terms of graphics and materiality. It was a chain admittedly but not in the McDonald's sense where every interior and shop front had the same identikit look from Land's End to John O'Groats. The point was emphasised subsequently by their conversion of Dr William Budd's nineteenth century home in Bristol. They created a chandelier using test tube pipettes, as an homage to his pioneering work in the prevention of typhoid.

The idea for Stiff + Trevillion was that to create a 'place', you needed to retain as much of the character of the existing premises as possible, and build on that, the details referring to the brand could then be layered onto this without detracting from it, optimising the process of image creation *Collage City*-style. "Transform the differences of each location into a positive" they argued, and you could make the most of each location, capturing its essential spirit. The differences in design terms within the chain's various outlets would be part of its selling point, what kept people interested. A good experience at Westfield in London would then resonate when the customer returned home to a find a Jamie's in their home town of Bath or Nottingham. It was, and remains, one of the core principles, which lies at the heart of the generation of architects like Mike and Andy, trained in *The Art of Memory* during the 1980s.

One of the most satisfying one-off restaurant commissions they worked on was Le Café Anglais, a large rotisserie restaurant in west London which was completed in 2007. This was very much a collaboration between Rowleigh Leigh, his business partner Charlie McVeigh, and the practice of Stiff + Trevillion, with Mike Stiff and Richard Blandy designing.

OPPOSITE Concept sketch by
Mike Stiff of Jamie's Italian, Bath,
showing a collage of materials
and finishes evoking the spirit of
a rustic food market in Lecche or
Bologna in Italy.

ABOVE Jamie's Italian. The
completed entrance area at the
Bath restaurant retains much
of the original concept sketch.

OPPOSITE Jamie's Italian, Bristol, showing a purpose designed chandelier made from test tubes—a reference to William Budd, who on this site in the nineteenth century, developed an inoculation for Typhoid, 2011.

LEFT Jamie's Italian, Aberdeen, using modular cut clay bricks to form screens around the main staircase, 2012.

RIGHT Jamie's Italian, Greenwich, with specially designed tiles for the floor and counter front, 2013. All of Stiff + Trevillion's designs for Jamie's Italians feature an original tile designed by the studio.

OPPOSITE Jamie's Italian, Liverpool, illustrating a laser-cut steel screen between the dining space and the bar, 2011.

ABOVE Jamie's Italian, Bristol. The wall cladding is made from cut Fletton bricks to provide an unusual texture at an economical price, 2011.

The idea of a rotisserie-based restaurant had been marinating in Leigh's mind for a couple of years. He had seen open air rotisseries in Normandy villages and was taken by the conviviality they engendered. According to him, not only was spit-roasting the best way to roast meat to perfection but a bank of rotisseries would inject a theatricality into any restaurant which could not be replicated in the home—this was the unique selling point of the concept.[11] Once again the key idea was pilfered from another culture, this time just across the channel, but was to be given a uniquely English edge. This synthesis would also help to sell the idea to London investors.

Then there was the space Leigh had ear-marked for the project. The idea for the architectural scheme started to take shape as soon as Mike set eyes on it. A former McDonald's fast-food outlet in the upper part of Whiteleys, a Victorian department store in Bayswater, which now functioned as a shopping mall. Only the external facades of the building's glory years remained but it was in a tourist hot-spot for those staying in the numerous cheap hotels in the area. It was hardly a high street location however, tucked away three storeys up at the top of the building, the project presented several challenges of which access was number one. Whiteleys closed early so customers wouldn't be able to access the restaurant through the mall and besides the concept was not suitable for a shopping mall type of environment. It needed to be pretty special to attract the high-end punters that Leigh needed to make it work financially and on the face of it at least, this was not a particularly suitable venue for anything, apart, perhaps, from a snooker hall.

On the plus side the actual space itself was to die for and pretty unique in any central London locality. Firstly there was the scale of it. Not only was it very large—7,000 square feet—but on their first visit they could just about discern that, hidden behind the false lowered ceilings of its former incarnation, it was lofty too, with four metre-high ceilings. On three sides it was surrounded by the most magnificent floor-to-ceiling Art Deco-style windows, which filled the great space with natural light, predominantly west-facing, the best for afternoons and evenings. According to Leigh, "it was a diamond shining in the rough".

The concept was already forming in the client's mind; he wanted the magnificent windows to be framed with glamorous curtains, to seat customers on soft leather banquettes and to introduce other elements from the tradition of the grand Parisian brasseries. There would be an open kitchen with a spectacular row of rotisseries as a focal point. Leigh had engaged with Stiff + Trevillion on an earlier project, which did not come to fruition, and had liked the practice's portfolio. The job was his, said Leigh, but first they needed to do some research together, so the next week the three of them, Leigh, McVeigh and Stiff, took off for a two-day trip around Paris. They visited every brasserie and grand restaurant they could find, they took tea at Café de Flore and Stiff sketched ideas for lights, mirrors and waiter's stations, romantically, on the back of envelopes. The team were inspired and the scheme started to take shape.

Leigh had been attracted to the Stiff + Trevillion portfolio for two reasons, firstly they appeared to understand the organic nature of a restaurant, that it had to be designed from the inside out, taking on-board a host of technical considerations. On one level a restaurant is the proverbial 'machine for eating in' and Mike and Richard Blandy had demonstrated this understanding right from that first restaurant project they had done for wagamama.

Secondly, they appreciated that modernism was not an ideology you had to be tied to on every project, as might be the case for a committed minimalist, for example. Mike and his team were flexible, their restaurants took their identity from the buildings within which they were located, and most importantly, from the client who had commissioned them. It was this notion of doing what the spaces asked for, avoiding preconceived ideas, working with the client rather than countering him with an assumption of superior knowledge, which won the practice the commission. Along with the excellent food and service, this sensitivity was ultimately what made the Le Café Anglais project such an enduring success.

An entrance lift was provided to connect a new street entrance to the upper floor restaurant, of which the tall, faceted windows dictated the feel of the room. A subtle 1930s feel was created using Bird's Eye maple, dark oak and bespoke lighting. The kitchen was open and formed a linear service run with the bar and bread station. Thus it connected the eating areas to the bar and the kitchen with a cool flow of seemingly functional events dressed-up in the drama of the design. Le Café Anglais became one of those iconic spaces in London, a room of such tremendous scale and depth it almost takes your breath away. As one colleague remarked to me recently, "I love this place—on the one hand it's like a vast ocean-going liner from the 1930s, on the other, it has intimate spaces carved-out for meetings with a lover or a small group of close friends. It is cosy and expansive at the same time."

The second consequence of the wagamama debacle was perhaps inevitable and was in some ways as important as the brochure, which found its way to Garry Hawkes and led to all these successful restaurant commissions. There was a launch event at the V&A museum, a big party with the attendees getting relaxed and convivial on good wine and canapés, circulating around the vast exhibition halls on the ground floor. Mike Stiff and John Pawson had both been invited and soon bumped into each other surrounded by the throng of artistic and cultural heavy-weights, influential movers and shakers, the type of people in front of whom, if you value your reputation, you should not make a scene.

Nevertheless, Mike was still bristling from the wagamama dispute and unburdened himself in no uncertain terms, accusing Pawson amongst other things of deliberately blurring the authorship of the wagamama scheme to his own advantage, Pawson responded in kind, it was a dramatic event to witness at such a highbrow affair.

Café Anglais, view of the main
dining space, a grand room with
a subtle combination of hard and
soft textures, in the best tradition
of the Parisian Brasserie, 2007.

The person who calmed the situation down was a property developer's agent called David Rosen. He had been largely responsible for reshaping Derwent London, the young and influential commercial property developers in London. He had also been involved with the launch of the 9H Gallery where, with Deyan Sudjic and Peter Murray at the helm, he had helped to initiate the new design and architecture journal *Blueprint*.

Mike apologised and harmony was restored for the rest of the evening. Rosen made a mental note to check out this passionate young man. It was, he confessed to Mike years later, something he rarely saw in an architect, and that, along with his portfolio, was what had attracted him to Stiff + Trevillion. Mike had often seen Rosen around town but they had never spoken. He was viewed by the architectural community as an agent of influence, a potential kingmaker, with an enthusiasm for architecture, unusual in the steely-hearted world of high finance. Sometime after the V&A bust-up Mike received a call from Rosen—he wanted to help the practice. They had lunch, and discussed a list of developers which might be useful to Stiff + Trevillion. This enabled a direct introduction to, amongst others, the head of developers at Derwent Valley. From this, a long and invaluable relationship with Simon Silver commenced.

— Be open to new influences, never stop learning. Sketch interesting details wherever you go, architecture is a vocation and travel broadens the mind.

— Be very careful when taking over where another practice has been before you, ensure there is clarity in terms of authorship and potential liability for poor design.

— Ensure maximum publicity when you have completed a project you are proud of, publicity is the life blood of this business; networking, both traditional and digital, is key.

— Use a good photographer, build a relationship with them so that they understand your work.

— Architecture is difficult without clear, unambiguous terms of reference. It requires certainty in order to make the right decision; a good client makes a good building.

— Specialising in a particular area of design is positive, but working across a number of different sectors, such as restaurants, schools, offices and hotels, enables diversification; when there is a recession in one area, you can cross over into another one.

151

— Being able to communicate to a diverse range of clients suggests that partners should be flexible, with the ability to communicate on an equal footing with anyone.

— Always know when it is time to give-up on a commission; if it is too stressful or out of your league, well-managed resignation can be the most honourable way to go.

CHAPTER 3 NOTES

1. IBA, Internationale Bauaustellung, Berlin, an urban renewal project initiated in 1979, completed in 1987, to coincide with the 750th anniversary of the founding of Berlin. Director Josef Paul Kleihues invited many international architects to build, including Peter Eisenman, Vittorio Gregotti, Herman Hertzberger, Hans Hollein, Arata Isozaki, Aldo Rossi and James Stirling.

2. *Prospect Magazine*, Issue 207, June 2013. Much of the text for the Berlin section was initiated from an article entitled "Margaret Thatcher: voice of the future", pp. 28–32.

3. Taken from *The Guardian* archive, 24 August 1990.

4. Clelland, Doug, "West Berlin 1984— the Milestone and the Millstone" in *Architectural Review*, September 1984, p. 19.

5. Polly Peck International was a small British textile company, which expanded rapidly in the 1980s and became a constituent of the FTSE 100 index, before collapsing in 1990 with debts of £1.3 billion.

6. Siemensstadt emerged when the company Siemens & Halske (established 1847) bought land in the area on the eastern side of the Spandau district of Berlin. It contains a mix of residential, civic and industrial buildings of high architectural quality from the 1930s.

7. Egham "A carefully crafted office develops the modern language of brick". Critique by Ellis Woodman, *Architecture Today*, Issue 106, pp. 20–24.

8. Eisenman, P, "Visions Unforlding— Architecture in the Age of Electronic Media" in Nesbitt, K, ed. *Theorising Architecture—a New Agenda for an Anthology of Architectural Theory*, New York: Princeton Architectural Press, 1996, p. 557.

9. "FLW: form follows feeling" in Wright, FL, *Frank Lloyd Wright—An Autobiography*, New York: Duel, Sloan and Pearce, 1943, pp. 13–14.

10. Conversations '09, quote from "Collaboration" essay by Rowley Leigh, from Stiff + Trevillion practice brochure, 2009.

Jamie's Italian, Portsmouth, 2010, with burnt wood bar fronts, shipping container walls and 'dazzleships' camouflaged ceiling—a reference to its quayside location.

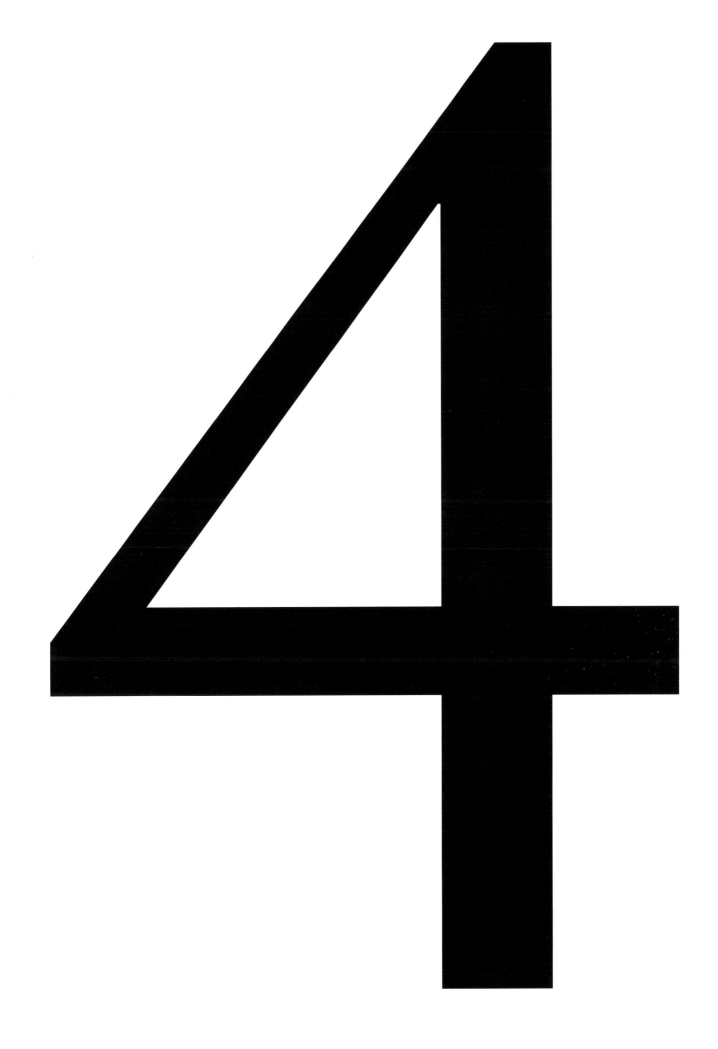

The 2000s

STABILITY AND GROWTH

Whether it is in their personal or in their business lives, some people know instinctively when it is time to move things forward with the next big push. On the other hand for many it is simply the happy conjunction of circumstances, an alignment of good fortune and professional discipline which dictates—it is simply the right time for things to happen. By the beginning of the new millennium, Stiff + Trevillion were definitely ready for the next stage in the evolution of their practice. They were financially stable, their design skills were now finely honed, indeed widely recognised within the industry. However the management of the business, both on the micro and on the larger strategic level, was still somewhat uncertain, occasionally haphazard. What key moves did they make to improve the performance of the business and optimise their undoubted design expertise? How did the business evolve from a small ten person practice at the turn of the century to a substantial 40 person practice in 2010?

On 11 September 2001 two hijacked passenger airliners crashed into the twin towers of New York's World Trade Centre. Both towers collapsed with the loss of thousands of lives, sending out great clouds of thick dust that covered buildings and people in the streets below. Lower Manhattan was evacuated and the iconic New York skyline changed forever. Minutes later in Washington DC a third hi-jacked aircraft crashed into the Pentagon, the heart of America's military machine. A fourth plane, believed to be heading for the presidential retreat at Camp David, crashed near Pittsburgh. The headline in *The Daily Telegraph* the following morning in the UK was "War on America".

PREVIOUS PAGE
1 Valentine Place.

OPPOSITE Footpatrol Soho. Trainers presented inside mesh school lockers help to give the brand a suitable, down-at-heel, faintly 'edgy' image, 2001.

Centres of government were evacuated throughout the United States and for a time the world's financial hub was paralysed when Wall Street closed down—share prices plunged around the world. President Bush was flown to a bunker in Nebraska before returning to the White House. He pledged to "hunt down and punish those responsible", saying no distinction would be made between the terrorists and those who harboured them. This event was to have enormously far-reaching consequences, not least the subsequent controversial invasion of Iraq, with Tony Blair wilfully insistent that the British Armed forces support the US military campaign without any real consideration of possible consequences for British citizens. The symbolism of 9/11 was clear to the global economic power brokers—this was an attack on the cradle of capitalism, a direct hit at the heart of the American Dream.

Then on 7 July 2005 a series of coordinated suicide attacks wreaked havoc during the morning rush hour in London. A group of home grown Islamic terrorists detonated four bombs, three in quick succession aboard London underground trains across the city and later a fourth on a double-decker bus in Tavistock Square. Apart from the four bombers themselves, 52 civilians were killed and over 700 more were seriously injured. As with New York post-9/11, the event merely strengthened the power of the City of London, and confirmed its status as a "world city".

Fortunately no-one within their immediate orbit was caught up in either the New York or the London attacks but for Stiff + Trevillion sitting in their Acklam Road studio watching the second plane hit the World Trade Center live on television, it was a stunning and terrifying turn of events nonetheless. Over the following months a sense of foreboding pervaded London, a sense that perhaps the capitalist world was not as stable as we had all assumed it to be, a questioning of values, priorities, and the whole capitalist ethos.

Mike, Andy and Richard had been working flat out for an entire decade, right up to the very last day of the old millennium. They had experienced extreme highs and lows during the 1990s, a lot of economic hardship at the mercy of the de-stabilising vagaries of the UK economy, and what they now felt they needed was above all a period of consolidation. Whilst they would have changed little of those early days in practice, they did often regret the stress that they had brought home to their families during those difficult times.

Added to this there was now the uncertainty of the shifting world order, attacks at the very heart of the Western economy with perhaps more to come—who could predict what might happen next in the 'Global Village'? The three partners therefore felt that they too had to take stock, not to stop working but to hunker down and restrict their focus, avoid risky decisions which might expose them and their employees in this new, turbulent reality. Andy and Mike in particular felt too that the time had come to slow down a little, to consider their work-life balance and to enjoy some head-space. The song "The Byrds" by Pete Seeger seemed to provide an appropriate *leitmotif* for the period:

To everything (Turn, Turn, Turn),
There is a season (Turn, Turn, Turn),
And a time to every purpose, under Heaven.

A time to build up, a time to break down,
A time to dance, a time to mourn,
A time to cast away stones, a time to gather stones together.[1]

In the bright dawn of the New Labour Government, which came to power in 1997, the British economy started to gather momentum. It is of some regret to Stiff + Trevillion that they were not really set-up during the early period of the decade to take advantage of the numerous millennium projects that were sprouting up all over Britain. However due to the fact that the practice remained relatively contained it enabled them to focus on their patrons in the world of commercial development and by the end of 2003 they consequently had the promise of significantly larger projects in the pipeline. They had decided early on not to take on public sector work and they had stuck to this pledge rigorously. Consequently, they ignored the announcement that the Olympic Games were scheduled to be held in London in 2012 and the vast capital investment which other similarly sized practices were aiming for in order to jump on the band wagon of public contracts. They concluded that this wasn't the direction they wanted the practice to take and stuck to their guns, continuing to focus on the possibilities of the commercial sectors which had become their speciality.

The four or five Stiff + Trevillion projects from the 1990s of which they were rightfully proud—Roke Manor and Egham (both office developments), plus the restaurant commissions of which wagamama, Satsuma and City Rhodes were the most high-profile—gave an interesting and rounded aspect to their portfolio. The expanding economy and the proliferation of easy money meant that work in the residential sector was now really taking off too and they were able to add several high-profile residential developments to the stable of their work: Hawkes House in Sussex and in 1999 a radical new studio/house in Copperfield Street SE1 for Keith Wainwright of Smile hairdressers. A clear range of three key specialisms was now emerging cementing the practice's reputation—commercial, residential and leisure (which focused mainly on restaurants).

This period of more circumspect growth gave Mike and Andy breathing space and the opportunity to make some natural, spontaneous connections which were to prove valuable—a sort of unforced networking. Mike found time to do some tutoring at the School of Architecture in Sheffield where he met two digitally savvy trainee architects, Ed Mullett and Dan Campbell, who strongly impressed him. These two young men would go on to become the foundation stones of the expanding practice's next generation studio team. Dan subsequently became a partner and Ed an associate. Later in 2005 Chris Eaton, another former Sheffield student recommended by Dan Campbell, came from a small Kensington practice to run the residential section as an Associate Director at Stiff + Trevillion.

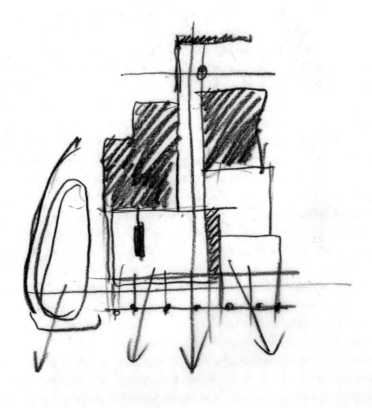

LEFT View of the Hawkes House from the south, with the pool room and the central glazed loggia clearly articulated as separate extensions onto the existing house, 1998.

RIGHT Hawkes House sketch proposals for client discussions on site, 1998. The plan indicates the two main ideas, a new north–south axis and views out to the Downs from the three primary spaces. The project was something of a labour of love, but was an award-winning residential scheme, which led to a number of new recommendations.

There was something about Sheffield students which suited them—they had some of the inspired lateral thinking of the Poly combined with a grounded, can-do work ethic which made them eminently employable.

The new century was a turning point for the practice. A lot of people they had previously charmed, irritated or impressed in years gone by were beginning to rise in influence within their own disparate worlds of commercial property development, and a certain showbiz-leisure orientated corporatism. Around this time Peter Murray's company Wordsearch was again enlisted to create a new corporate identity for the business. Importantly he fashioned the portfolio of Stiff + Trevillion completed projects into a small but exquisitely-designed brochure. (Mike and Andy's early pledge to always have their key projects photographed professionally was critical to this make-over. They were very aware that hard-won, successfully completed commissions were the calling card for the next job and that they needed to make the most of each and

every one). The brochure was to prove as key to their future success as the slick, up-graded website in promoting the practice's profile. Slowly the business was developing a more refined image which intuitively complemented their architectural values, something that was to prove crucial during the next stage of growth. Stiff + Trevillion's identity was solidifying around old-school values in terms of working practices and client care, complemented by a distinctively modern kind of architecture focused on their three distinctive areas of expertise.

DAVID ROSEN, SIMON SILVER AND THE DEVELOPER'S NETWORK

David Rosen, was very much of the same lineage and was attracted to the partners for that reason. A prominent commercial agent and someone with significant powers of patronage, he has been responsible for the promotion of numerous up-and-coming architectural practices often recommending left-of-field suggestions to larger commercial sector developers like Derwent London and Helical Bar. He had first come across Mike at the infamous party at the V&A in the 1990s where he had locked horns with John Pawson over the authorship of wagamama—it was Rosen who had calmed the situation preventing an escalation of the feud. (Indeed to this day Mike and John Pawson, both west Londoners, get on well.) The escapade had made its mark on Rosen, and he was drawn to this passionate young architect, interested to see what drove and inspired him. Over the ensuing decade or so the two had become friends, attending social events together and generally enjoying each other's company. Rosen also trusted Mike and felt that he was a man he could do business with.

Like Mike, Rosen was something of an architecture 'anorak', not only eminently knowledgeable about good contemporary design but also with an innate appreciation for classic modernist architecture. Unusually for a developer at that time, he firmly believed that if you used better designers you would get better financial returns. Building commissions were fundamentally commercial decisions but they could also speak of a deep cultural awareness and the wish to promote innovative ideas and new talent. Importantly for Mike, Andy and Richard, during the 1980s Rosen had seen through the shallow facade of the Neoclassicists and recognised that architecture did not need to be retro to be populist and commercially successful.

Out of the blue Rosen called Mike and suggested they have lunch. In conversation it transpired that they held similar views about the problems and the opportunities presented by London's evolving architecture and it was a task that both men took seriously. They were also both part of the immediate post-war generation who had vivid memories of passing bomb sites around London as children and were aware of the need for historical knowledge to inform the new architecture necessary to revive the city. In addition they agreed that this knowledge was not enough on its own but needed to be abstracted and expressed through contemporary forms.

Wordsearch designed the first Stiff + Trevillion brochure, usually referred to as the "purple book". Peter Murray came up with a more challenging title, describing their work as being "A Modern Tradition".

The Czech Embassy in
Notting Hill Gate, by RMJM,
1970, admired by Mike Stiff
and David Rosen.

David Rosen had been brought-up in St John's Wood and whenever he
and Andy Trevillion get together they still reminisce about the shops and
music venues they had frequented back in the day. However, it was Mike
with his deep affection for all kinds of architecture with whom Rosen
really bonded. Mike describes a moment when their mutual passion
for iconic mid-century design came to the fore. They had attended an
Architecture Club meeting and were walking back through Kensington
Palace Gardens, both heading towards the tube station. They stopped
at the Czech Embassy, a forgotten piece of expressive modernism in
coarse white concrete with accentuated pre-fabricated concrete bays
rising up above the street at first and second floor levels.[2] There must
have been something Cold War about the creative tension between
the roughness of the concrete and the smoothly etched glass of this
assertive piece of Brutalism (designed in 1966 but completed in 1970),
which fascinated them. "They were so certain and had the power to
express the simplicity of a good idea through their architecture in those
days", Mike remarked, reflecting on his travels in East Germany. It was
experience that Rosen had been unaware of but which now intrigued
him. They both extolled the virtues of the stacked glass sign, admiring
the building's finish which had weathered so well over time. It was a
powerful moment when their two imaginations seemed conjoined, it was
to prove a lasting creative relationship.

A few weeks later Rosen recommended Stiff + Trevillion to Simon Silver,
a property developer involved in many central London sites. In 1980,
along with partner John Burns, Silver had started a small investment
company, Derwent London. A youthful Silver had experienced a
'eureka' moment of his own when he had taken the potentially risky
decision to appoint two young architects who had just left Richard
Rogers. Troughton McAslan then expertly transformed a redundant

warehouse in Islington (like Mike and Andy, they had been exhibited in the 40 under 40 exhibition during the 1980s). It was the catalyst Silver needed to get seriously interested in architecture. For Silver and Burns, what the young practice did was transformative, modifying for the better not just the building but also the rental value. It opened their eyes to the value of good contemporary architecture, and from that moment on, Silver became immersed in the culture of architecture, learning from his stable of new young practices as well as from his own academic engagement in the art of architecture.

Simon Silver has over the years developed a keen interest in art, architecture and design. He is not trained but the culture and spirit of design is in his blood. According to Stiff, this is what differentiates Derwent London from other developers. Most will have a corporate art collection for investment purposes, but Silver and Derwent find new artists in the same way they find architects, to somehow incorporate their work into the building; they simply love exploring the most contemporary of ideas, and admire the unique ways in which certain artists are able to evoke the spirit of the age through their work. They are patrons of the arts but have no interest in collecting art and hiding it away in a museum—for Silver art and architecture are complimentary, and the best gallery to view it is a new building where people come into contact with the art everyday, perhaps whilst passing through an entrance area on their way into the office. For example Hugo Dalton is a young artist 'discovered' by Simon who specialises in art projects for buildings. Dalton has worked on two significant projects with Stiff + Trevillion at the suggestion of Silver. It remains an ongoing relationship.

Often in this world, the development process can last for many years, and can be full of potential conflict, there must be respect, a strong sense of creative empathy and excellent personal relationships in order for it to all go smoothly. According to Mike, if you really like a client you deliver your best work, although it is probably more about mutual respect and the exchange of knowledge that keeps the relationship fresh.

A few weeks after first meeting with Silver, the practice was briefed about a small site in London's Jermyn Street, which was home to a dated 1970s office building (ironically one of Chapman and Taylor's better designs, the practice Mike had worked for during his immediate post-PCL days). As it was their first for Derwent, Stiff + Trevillion went to town on the pitch, developing a very plausible sketch scheme complete with perspective views of the key interiors. Included in the team was a young Ed Mullett who had recently been recruited from the Sheffield School of Architecture. Mullett produced a set of stunning computer generated images, which in particular focused on the entrance using a cool, restrained palette of materials which were inspired by their minimalist restaurant designs of that period—wagamama and Satsuma. It was the beginning of a strong and consistent design ethos and established a systematic working pattern for these types of projects.

Mike Stiff recalls that time very clearly. The team had worked heroically to get the design drawings ready in time for the presentation, burning the midnight oil, not a good strategy perhaps, however they had no choice, at that time they simply did not have enough people to pull-in for the intense design and production required to meet Derwent's deadline. The presentation was to Simon and David Rosen, who perhaps realised that the team had worked hard to get to where they had in the time period. In addition for Mike it was a very special time, on 11 September 2000, the day before the presentation, his wife, Marianne, went into labour and was taken into hospital expecting their first baby. Their son Oskar was safely delivered at 11pm. Mike left his sleeping wife and son in time to grab a few hours rest, have a quick shower and rush across to Derwent's offices for a 10am presentation. Bleary eyed he explained the events of the previous night, delivered a good presentation and sensed that it had all gone pretty well, there was real empathy between the two professional teams. It was the start of a beautiful friendship.

This particular project did not proceed, however Stiff + Trevillion had impressed the developer. Simon and Mike soon discovered a mutual passion for a particular type of architecture, a sort of mid-century modern, exemplified by the likes of Mies van der Rohe, Frank Lloyd Wright and Richard Neutra. The relationship developed further during the following two years, with David Rosen continuing to champion Stiff + Trevillion's merits. Derwent finally came up with an appropriate vehicle, appointing Stiff + Trevillion in 2003 to undertake a rolling

refurbishment of Morley House in Regent Street. This was very much a breakthrough commission.

Stiff + Trevillion and Derwent have worked together fairly consistently ever since, producing a sequence of significant built projects of the highest quality. For Mike the great thing is that they both enjoy the conversations and research around the development of any new project, they are now great friends and enjoy similar tastes. They are constantly looking for something new to set their latest project apart. For example, when developing a new office building in Islington in 2010, Mike suggested they use a particularly unusual brick from Denmark. The team spent a rewarding time visiting the Petersen brick factory near Copenhagen before deciding to proceed (they stayed in the SAS hotel designed by Arne Jacobson, another Silver favourite). A brave move perhaps but a joint decision based on a solid and mutual understanding of the implications of this novel material. Every Derwent project is undertaken in this spirit curiosity and limited experimentation.

STÜSSY AND JAMIE'S ITALIAN

By 2002 Stiff + Trevillion had completed their year of taking stock and they were ready to move on up a gear. In the 1980s Mark Eden, a friend of Mike's from Newbury had introduced them to his employer Keith Wainwright of Smile hairdressers. They had completed a studio-house for Keith in Copperfield Street in 1999 and through that successful commission had come into contact with a number of his more influential clients. For Stiff + Trevillion, Wainwright proved to be an important addition to their network. In 2001 Keith introduced them to Michael Kopelman, a Smile client who was looking for an architect.

Kopelman, along with partners Simon Porter and Fraser Cooke, wanted to develop a group of youth-orientated fashion outlets in the West End. On the basis of his first visit to Wainwright's concrete house in Copperfield Street, he asked Mike to design the first Stüssy store in the UK in Earlham Street, Covent Garden. Stüssy was one of the cool new millennium brands he represented, which celebrated the then popular West Coast skate boarding culture. Slightly leftfield for Stiff, the commission was taken on-board as an imagined youthful world of unnerving, almost subversive conjunctions using street architecture in a subtly choreographed setting. With the aim of throwing the visitor-off balance, as if on a wobbly skateboard, Stiff introduced a hyperbolic sloping floor of birch ply divided down the centre, with one ramp curving into a display shelf. At the front of the store there was a full-height window with a sliding glazed door bringing the street bustle right into the internal space. His concept was that when selling street fashion it made sense to bring the street, metaphorically, into the shop. The design was an immediate success clearly the interior extended the brand: the architectural narrative brought newly associated themes cleverly into focus using conceptual ideas which the clients instinctively responded to.

OPPOSITE Copperfield Street apartment for Keith Wainwright, interior view of the principal staircase—an integral element within the narrative.

ABOVE The Copperfield Street apartment, the main staircase; the project was nicknamed the "concrete house" by its satisfied client.

RIGHT Copperfield Street apartment showing the original pre-cast concrete portal frame in dramatic juxtaposition with the smooth new plaster walls, 1999.

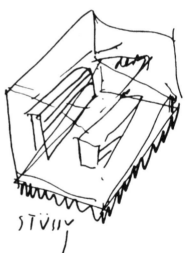

The next Kopelman commission was Footpatrol, a retail outlet selling high fashion sneakers, like women's boxing boots commissioned by Adidas from Stella McCartney, a snip at £290 a pair. The challenge was how to turn a 46 square metre tanning parlour in a Soho alley into a destination store. Rather than playing down the faintly shady context, after some deliberation Stiff adopted an alienating, post-industrial feel with shoes displayed in cages like puppies in a pet shop using mesh school lockers. The shop counter and floor was skinned in a flecked-rubber composite, originally intended for basketball courts and appropriately made of recycled sneakers. "It's intended to be an almost unfriendly, very industrial atmosphere that reminds me of a school, or a benefits office or an off-license in a dodgy area" says Stiff.[2] So successful was the store that for the first few months the queues of sneaker aficionados seeking limited edition footwear was so long that staff had to impose a ticket system to control entry. The crazy cost of the product was perhaps a symbolic representation of the times but Mike's design was clever and almost anti-money with its use of cheap, low-budget finishes. For a while it became the essence of noughties street culture.

Further commissions followed along similar highly thematic lines, particularly in the restaurant sector, which expanded significantly over the following few years, with the practice completing landmark projects such as the St Alban restaurant in Regent Street for Chris Corbin and Jeremy King. Eating, like fashion, was an all-round sensory experience and the environment was as important as the food and the service provided. Based on their almost unique expertise, towards the end of

2006, Stiff + Trevillion were approached by the celebrity chef Jamie Oliver who had financial backing to develop a new chain of Italian themed restaurants called Jamie's Italian. As these would not be one-off's, the client recognised the importance of good design, they were prepared to pay well for a comprehensive service which enabled Stiff + Trevillion to fully resource the design team and to really work hard on the design.

The germ of the idea came as a result of the early discussions they had with Jamie Oliver and his team, Simon Blagden and Matt Utber. Oliver was informed and enthusiastic about the architecture and wanted each restaurant to become the "local Italian", where food, produce and the process of cooking would become central to the design and to the interior spaces. The interior architecture would represent the values and style of Jamie Oliver without raising expectations that Jamie would actually be in the kitchen. Richard Blandy's technical knowledge of restaurant design was by this time comprehensive. He had naturally assumed the mantle of the head of the leisure sector within Stiff + Trevillion, and felt that it

OPPOSITE TOP The Stüssy store, Earlham Street, Covent Garden, in central London, 2000.

OPPOSITE BOTTOM Stüssy concept sketch by Mike Stiff, which proved to be an evocative image, appealing to the client during the preliminary presentations.

ABOVE Footpatrol Soho.

was important to ensure that each new restaurant would be designed as a distinctive one-off interior, which respected the original building and its location. This meant that for each a new design team was brought in, the one constant would always be Blandy, to ensure that significant technical requirements were always consistently adhered to.

They considered developing the difference as a series of moods inspired by the regions of Italy, for example the warm ochres and reds of Tuscany compared to the crisp yellows and blues of Naples. Each would be used for different rooms or building types. The Oliver image was very much contemporary and of the minute, almost youthful in its take on food and the stylistic flavour which goes with it, this they felt was part of the allure. Of course rustic might suit some sites, for others 2010 Vespa cool would be more appropriate. The mood colours worked to a certain extent on the first prototype restaurant in Bath, with the top floor terrace level in bright blues and yellows and the ground floor snug in cosy ochres and reds, subsequently they had to concentrate more on tailoring each design specifically for its location, rather than adopting the same branded approach across the estate.

As we write the practice has completed ten Jamie's Italians across the country. The first in Bath, in a building that is part new, part eighteenth century Georgian, has been a tremendous success—the restaurant uses the range of different spaces to its advantage developing a particular Italian style for each. Colour is used to accentuate mood in two of the spaces. This complexity and eclecticism became a thematic that was fully explored in all of the follow-on restaurants with the use of a variety of natural materials, marble timber and steel which used side by side give off a richly vibrant effect. Italian staple food is displayed openly as part of the décor. Great rounds of Parmigiano Reggiano cheese are lined up along the counter and huge legs of cured ham and pork hang tantalisingly above, the busy chefs each having been coached personally by Oliver, enliven the proceedings performing their magic in the open kitchen immediately behind the counter. It has the feel of an Italian market, albeit a confined one.

This type of small but high profile project was now fundamental to the Stiff + Trevillion brand and has made a significant difference to their bottom line. The Jamie's chain continued to expand following the Lehman's crash of 2008 seemingly oblivious to the recession (customers viewing it as an economical alternative to the higher-end restaurants), which helped Stiff + Trevillion to weather the storm. These design intensive jobs also illustrate the inherently flexible approach Stiff + Trevillion have developed. They do not have a house-style as such. Whilst they are very aware of trends and fashions and are able to work flexibly with each client, sensitive to their individual needs always developing the design concepts on their terms. From the most conservative, 'pin-stripe' office block in the City to a house for a hairdresser, they could adapt and produce something appealing, intriguing yet inherently appropriate within the confines of the context. It was a defining period in terms of

The St Alban Restaurant, Regent Street, for Chris Corbin and Jeremy King with artwork by Michael Craig-Martin, 2006.

their image and reputation within the industry. They were seen as sound, a serious, professional London practice guaranteed to deliver, an outfit which combined valuable practical experience with wide-ranging and eclectic architectural knowledge. Most importantly, they were talented designers who were able to reflect and anticipate the *zeitgeist*. They were building important and influential contacts within London's commercial sector, optimistically dreaming about altogether larger commissions. Now they interviewed the clients as much as the clients interviewed them but they were small, they didn't need a large expensive office just yet.

ACKLAM ROAD STUDIOS AND QUALITY ASSURED

In 1993, they had moved from the High Street Kensington offices to a small mews building in a grungy but increasingly fashionable part of Notting Hill. They had been assisted in this decision by a timely intervention. Andrew Eden a friend of Mike's from his PCL days, had offered them the office just off Westbourne Grove. A 'mates' deal with no long-term lease it seemed like a risk-free economical arrangement, it was cheap—it would allow them to take what seemed like one huge overhead out of the financial equation. They jumped at the chance to leave behind the High Street Kensington shopping street location and move into something altogether less conventional. 4 Westbourne Grove Mews was a small two-storey building sandwiched between a launderette and an importer of African pottery, opposite a busy car maintenance garage. Totalling about 1,000 square feet it was a tight squeeze for their ten employees but it was big enough for the time being. It became their office base for the next phase in the evolution of the practice, until 2003 when they finally felt absolutely confident that expansion was safe and desirable.

By 2003, the practice was bulging at the seams, finding it difficult to fit into Westbourne Grove Mews and the additional space they had hired across the road above the garage. However their experience of the late 1980s recession and the hard slog of the Berlin project, left Stiff + Trevillion risk averse. Understandably they were nervous about expensive office leases, keen not to borrow and expand. Although they had now cleared their debt, its memory lingered, stalking them in the background like the ghost of Banquo. They now understood that what was most critical for the future of their business was the level of architectural efficiency they were able to bring to the market place. The reputation of the practice had spread and it was acknowledged that they had design flair in spades, but now they felt that they had also acquired the requisite technical acumen which they had lacked somewhat during the early days and they wanted to capitalise on this. Whilst they were still a little short on business management know-how in some respects, they believed that they would continue to build on this as long as they stayed sharp and focused on design. For Mike, this meant remaining small and agile, at least for a while.

They also decided on a development strategy for contained, steady growth. Everything they built henceforth, particularly the commercial work where they hoped to see further expansion, would have to be considered and undertaken in clear professional teams. They would concentrate on resourcing each project with the appropriate head count. Winning the commission was still the first priority but equally important was selecting the right team for each job in terms of size and experience. If it was not possible to get that balance right within their small practice, then they would walk away from the project, or recommend it to another practice, particularly if the profit margins were unpredictable. All three partners agreed there must be no more over-leveraged, under-managed expansion. Taking on too much work was as bad as having too little work.

Naturally, above all, each project must be well-designed, however Stiff + Trevillion were now much more conscious that it must also be delivered on time and within budget, and inevitably to achieve this some concessions would be required along the way. Building is unpredictable and people's views change. If the budget or the time frame are running short, compromises in design detail are often required. Like a piece of wet clay pushed from one direction and then from the other, the overall form of the design changes and evolves. In their early years enthusiasm and the arrogance of youth had led them to believe that the architect always knew best. Now their attitudes had changed significantly, approaching their 40s they were more mature in outlook, realistic in their expectations and much more responsible. They re-thought their approach to commissions and their fee structure in a way that would anticipate the need for changes to the contract drawings to cover any required amendments during the design period. They factored in a degree of controlled modification during the actual build phase, to take into account the fact that clients so often view things differently when the reality can be seen and felt as construction progresses. Such was the depth of experience they could now draw upon they found to their relief that these changes could actually be incorporated with very little diminution of quality. Indeed, Mike and Andy realised that often even better design outcomes emerged following these enforced budgetary compromises or clients' amendments. It was all about a certain state of mind, a flexible, altogether more adaptable approach, a concept they had learned little about at college but had absorbed on the job. They now felt confident that from these fundamental principles of flexibility and quality assured, word would get around and further commissions would follow.

A certain amount of PR was still required to keep things ticking over and their name on potential clients' radars, but the partners were now finding this was less of a problem than in the previous decades. During this time their respective roles evolved further and Andy became in a sense Mike's anchor, the person who in particular ensured that the finances were under control, the bank was happy, the client's contractual needs were addressed and cash flow was maintained. It was almost as if all his early background working for Dicky Dirt's, seemingly unrelated to architecture, had given him valuable real life experience which was now proving to be precious. Whereas Mike's life was consumed by architecture in its purest sense, Andy had a broader, more grounded view

of the world and of the business. Richard Blandy, the third partner, was in the same camp, keeping an eye on the bottom line, the memory of the lock-out of 1989 still vivid and tending to colour strategic decisions. Trevillion and Blandy urged steady growth, nothing too risky: there was a sensible balance to be struck between being over-cautious and expanding too quickly. One Swallow doesn't make a summer, one medium-sized job does not make a sustainable three-year plan. The practice needed to stay small and grow at a sustainable pace, if the three were to be able to sleep at night.

Andy, and to a lesser extent Richard, largely undertook the bread-and-butter commissions which provided their staple income in times when the high-profile projects were thin on the ground. In any practice there are jobs which are hardly seen, the 'background buildings' which form the grain of the city, they were both willing to field these when Mike was otherwise occupied. The two were now also very adept at building, well-versed in constructional know-how, and could act as technical gate-keepers, advising when there was a misplaced DPC or commenting on the position of a fire escape, for example. Not exactly glamorous work but an essential requirement of any design practice nevertheless. When tasked with turning up for an important pitch with a sketch proposal which covers all bases, they were always there to provide instant technical adjustments so that what they showed was plausible. That way the drawings provided no distractions from the main task of selling the primary conceptual idea. The mantra which had been drummed into them by Doug Clelland at the Poly, kept coming back to them, communicate the main idea.

RICHARD COOK AND DESIGNERS GUILD

The Keith Wainwright connection brought them into contact with Kim Sion, who ran Smile Management, an off-shoot of the hairdresser's which was a high-end fashion photography agency. Kim was based in a stylish, purpose-designed industrial studio backing onto the railway tracks running into Paddington Station. She had decided to move the business on and offered to assign her lease to Stiff + Trevillion. It was a timely offer, the mews had served them well, but it was time to expand and consolidate and this 2000 square foot unit was right for Stiff + Trevillion. In January 2004 they moved to the new studio on Acklam Road (where the Notting Hill Carnival riots started in 1976).

They had now doubled their workspace and were working together in the open-plan space. They equipped their new home with Vitra furniture so that on entering the offices the client would get a sense of the financial health and design ambition of their business. It was all a far cry from the slightly shabby studio in Westbourne Grove Mews where they had to make-do with desks made from door blanks. Now they were financially robust and confident that their expansion plans were soundly based on larger new commercial commissions rather than on tentative expectations. The move to Acklam Road was timely. There is nothing

173

Notting Hill Carnival, where, in August 1977, poor crowd control by the police resulted in two days of rioting, which started on Acklam Road. Here the police run past a Mister Whippy ice cream van, they have no riot gear, and can be seen holding onto their helmets, carrying truncheons like the Keystone Cops. The Westway is in the background.

Hammerson HQ, Grosvenor Street, London, 2006. View of the reception, designed by Mike Stiff and Dan Campbell.

clients such as Simon Silver, or Jon Emery of Hammerson like more than coming to the architect's studio, looking at samples, seeing models of other projects in the office, and simply hanging out. Slowly but surely, as the work materialised they expanded from around 20 employees by 2006. This was something of a boom time for them as they could see the three sectors growing and with improved turnover, the business was becoming more profitable. Restaurants and residential were experiencing something of a boom, and now the commercial clients were beginning to recognise their expertise.

Three years before Stiff + Trevillion took the lease on her offices, Kim Sion, who according to Mike is a London 'hipster', and knew a lot of people in the fashion and music world introduced them to a developer friend who was experiencing some difficulties with a west London site. He had an architect on board but was struggling to get permission to develop it. This was a backlot in Latimer Road, a stone's throw from where Mike and his own family lived in W10. It was on one of those shabby London streets which was reminiscent of parts of US suburbia, a mixture of undistinguished Victorian terraced housing and low-grade, incoherent light industrial 'sheds', with a railway track running behind them. The elevated section of the Westway made an abrupt termination to a street which in better days had run unimpeded all the way down to the leafy splendour of Holland Park.

However when Mike went to see the site and met the developer, Richard Cook, two worlds suddenly and explosively collided. Unexpectedly the site really excited him, for some reason its challenges—the narrow street frontage, the low-rise context and even the fact that it was all a bit down-at-heel—sparked his imagination. "To make something beautiful there, I knew I was going to have to make the best building in the street", recalls Mike,

In that sort of context you are setting the standard, initially its quite daunting... but once you get into it, you can enthuse the owner with a mixture of images and words which can paint a three-dimensional picture—it's where architects with all their training can see ahead, they have vision. Most clients can't look at plans, its meaningless to them, a good architect brings a three-dimensional imagination to bear... often it's the site itself that sparks your enthusiasm and click, off you go....

Perhaps, also because it was so close to home, it meant a lot to him on an emotional basis. In a sense he was offering a radical improvement to his own territory through this development and for that reason it was special.

It was certainly a challenge as Cook needed to fulfil its rental potential to make the project stack-up for him financially, they had to work hard to maximise the square footage within its low-scale residential surroundings. Luckily the developer and the architect hit it off instantly and Stiff + Trevillion took over the project. Mike worked his magic developing a sophisticated scheme which was speedily

approved for planning. The piece has been described as "a jewel in a sea of mediocrity" but perhaps a more appropriate soubriquet would be "background architecture", the kind of creative but harmonious building which forms the back-drop of an evolving, vital city, the kind of architecture in which Stiff + Trevillion excel, in this case with some very neat touches like carving-out a stunning internal courtyard which creates its own sense of place.[3] It is certainly the best building in the street now and in time it will hopefully attract other high quality contemporary in-fills which knit seamlessly into the existing urban grain in the same way and help to mend the streetscape.

Number 3 Latimer Place was let-out almost as soon as it was finished to Designers Guild, a successful interiors and fabrics retailer, a high-grade tenant bringing employment and status to an almost forgotten part of town. Richard Cook the young developer could not have been happier. An Arts graduate from Edinburgh with a more than passing interest in architecture, he had subsequently studied for an MBA in business management founding his own property company at the age of 30. When he met Mike in 2003 he had discovered someone who was both creative and, being 15 years older, had the type of experience in the London property world which was like gold-dust. Mike and Andy were generous and wise in the advice they gave to Richard over the following years and developed a sound friendship with him, often going salmon

ABOVE AND OVERLEAF
3 Latimer Place, the conversion and extension of a redundant industrial building into the corporate HQ of Designers Guild, 2003.

fishing together in Scotland, and meeting for dinner regularly to exchange news and to keep up with family events. Richard would often pop in to the Notting Hill offices on his way to a site. During these visits he sometimes picked up on bits and pieces about how the practice was run. An extremely bright individual, he started to feed critical observations back to Mike, in the most diplomatic of ways, helping him to see where improvements might be made. Eventually in 2006, the partners asked Cook if he would become the chairman of Stiff + Trevillion.

Ever since the time Stiff + Trevillion had bought into the John Stiff Partnership in 1985, Andy had taken on the task of upgrading the practice's management structures and being generally responsible for the administration systems. For example in the early 1990s he had brought in basic accounting software to facilitate the everyday book-keeping, identifying where the biggest costs lurked, keeping abreast of the digital processes, dealing with employment contracts which were a potential minefield. Small-scale architectural offices rarely deal with business administration procedures effectively, and during the early days of the noughties Stiff + Trevillion was no exception. However, Andy was critically aware that for the business to prosper someone had to take responsibility for this, overseeing everything from invoicing to timesheets, payroll, archiving and contract management. Mike had a quick mind but this was an area he could barely engage with. Besides he had enough on his plate on the design side.

However, Andy was conscious that he himself lacked the necessary business knowledge where certain critical decisions were concerned. He was also painfully aware of the limited understanding they had about business management compared to the depth of their experience of building. While they had hired a good accountant to advise on tax planning, profit and loss and cash flow, he couldn't teach them how to increase their profit margins. They didn't yet have the resources to employ a full-time, high-level business administrator and besides, where would they find such a qualified pro-active person to move the business forward?

When Richard Cook appeared on the scene the practice was suddenly able to tap into a whole new seam of business expertise. Here was someone who understood the development world and had one of the best business brains Andy had encountered. He soon proved to be exactly the guiding hand they needed, providing inestimable insights and precise, targeted advice just when they needed it. He was proactive, prompting the partners to implement profit and loss projections, to keep on top of their cash-flow and to generally tighten-up their administrative systems from top to bottom. Cook was also astute at timing the PR needed to push the practice's profile and at assuaging the potential of commissions. He guided the business through a maze of competing priorities and helped them to identify where profit margins were worthy of consideration and where they were negligible, enabling them to evaluate more effectively whether certain jobs of a particular size and complexity should be avoided or embraced. He steered the development of the business throughout the

ABOVE TOP 3 Latimer Place a view of the internal courtyard, a haven of tranquility in north-west London, W10.

ABOVE BOTTOM Concept sketch illustrating 3 Latimer Place, the first, and most successful, collaboration with developer Richard Cook.

OPPOSITE View south across the courtyard, with the Westway in the distance.

crucial period of growth in the step-up from a small practice struggling to invest and develop, to one which was profitable and resourceful and able to lure in high-quality employees and collaborators.

By the mid-2000s Stiff + Trevillion had become a well-known, tightly run London-based practice of serious architects with an enviable reputation for the quality of their design, working for high-profile clients such as Hammerson, Derwent and Workspace. They had stuck to their early principles of preferring to collaborate with people they cared about and were inspired by, pooling intellectual resources in pursuit of a set of shared ideals where good architecture and personal loyalty went hand-in-hand, people like Doug Clelland, David Rock, Peter Murray, David Rosen, Simon Silver and Richard Cook. Finally between 2004 and 2008 things became markedly easier for the partners as the soaring British economy propelled the growing practice up to the next level at dizzying speed.

PORTOBELLO DOCK

Simon Silver, of Derwent London, states that "Architecture is essential to our business, if you get the architect wrong you get the scheme wrong."[4] Clearly architects have been central to the whole development formula of the company. Very early on in its evolution Silver commented that they had latched on to a stable of younger, aspirational architects, hungry practices without big egos who were keen to prove their mettle. They wanted to work with firms who were genuinely interested in architecture and

322 High Holborn, London, WC1. Office re-fit for developers Derwent London, showing the reception desk in opal glass with feature back lighting, 2004.

understood the real meaning of modernism in a pluralistic age. As he states categorically, "We want our buildings to be original, different and cutting edge without being gimmicky".[5] The profile of the type of practice they were looking for summed up Stiff + Trevillion to a 'T'.

The second commission that Simon gave them was 322 High Holborn in 2004. Comprising the radical repositioning of an interesting but tired 1970s office building, the project incorporated those characteristic Stiff + Trevillion design flourishes which lifted them above the ordinary. For example elegance and relaxed modernism are eased into the entrance areas and common spaces at 322 High Holborn where they carved out a double-height space with a mezzanine from the original low, squat porch, enervating the entrance into something which is smoothly civic, flows from the street and feels appropriate to the users.

Similarly at Morley House they informed the entrance sequence with three completely disparate materials, smooth warm walnut cladding, pristine white illuminated render on the walls and Italian basalt on the floors, touches which lend the area a sense of purpose and cool efficiency—clear, clean architecture to promote clear, clean thinking. At the Morley House entrance lobby there are a pair of Art Deco-style columns supporting the structure which are accentuated to meld an iconic historical reference into the modernity of the piece. In each project there is a surety of purpose which suggests that the skills Stiff + Trevillion had honed during the execution of numerous detailed and nuanced restaurant interiors and residential projects, have produced an important cross-fertilisation of ideas. Their ability to use apposite detail and lighting to create critical ambience makes for humane but also functional places, as effective in an office building as in an eatery. It was this awareness which played such a vital role in these early commercial successes.

Their impressive work on these two projects gave Simon Silver the confidence to consider Stiff + Trevillion for a prestigious new-build much closer to home. Mike in particular had become quite close to Simon Silver and had accompanied him in 2003 to look at the Virgin Records HQ at Portobello Dock just off Harrow Road in west London. It was an interesting site on the edge of Derwent's furthest acceptable location and just round the corner from Stiff + Trevillion's offices. They had completed a number of mixed-use and office developments in the area, including Latimer Road which was only a ten-minute walk away. It was their locale, they were particularly fond of Maxwell Fry's white-rendered stucco block of Modernist social housing, Kensal House, 1937, almost adjacent to the site to the south. Mike knew instantly it was another of those projects that would excite him. Within five minutes of arriving on that first site visit he was already trying to fit the pieces together logically to form a coherent masterplan and deriving immense satisfaction from the challenge. The first preliminary feasibility study was completed in January 2004.

Having started his business on a barge moored in Little Venice, Richard Branson always had a fondness for the Grand Union Canal and in the

182

ABOVE Morley House, their first office re-fit for Derwent, with the main reception area showing two original marble columns which had been hidden behind plasterboard since the 1960s, 2002–2003.

OPPOSITE The White Building, Portobello Dock, north Kensington which had originally been Richard Branson's Virgin Records HQ.

1980s had acquired the early-Victorian Kensal House (which was listed as Grade II), on the Harrow Road, together with the Canal Dock to the south, and linked the two sites with a new pedestrian bridge. This became the Virgin Records HQ until it was sold to EMI in the late 1990s. Being on the edge of the Royal Borough of Kensington and Chelsea, (and partly straddling Westminster on the north), the south-western end of the site felt like the main point of access to the borough. As with Latimer Place but on a much larger scale, this was another opportunity to use a new development to improve the spatial quality of the entire locality, with potential to raise property values and improve the local infrastructure. The North Kensington planning team were very happy to have a design-orientated developer such as Derwent London on-board and knew Stiff +

Trevillion from other projects in the area. This gave them confidence to trust that the commission would turn out well.

Although Stiff + Trevillion changed uses and enhanced the aesthetic of the northern site most of the new development work was undertaken on the south side of the canal. The overall idea was to retain the campus concept of a mixed-use estate of buildings which share semi-public spaces at ground level. There are three main buildings which comprise the development: the Canal Building which uses the trapezoidal gateway site to the west, Portobello Lofts to the east, a remodelled office building from the 1980s which was skilfully adapted into penthouse flats, and the White Building to the north of the canal, a group of existing stucco buildings which were simply remodelled and refurbished to provide 25,000 square feet of new office space and seven apartments. The entire area was completely re-landscaped to provide parking space and gardens that were orientated towards the canal which quietly flows beneath the Westway towards Paddington Basin.

The Canal Building is the most dramatic of the three and comprises a new six-storey office building, a free-standing structure which nonetheless engages with the industrial history of the area, moulding itself to the eccentrically shaped site whose contours give the building its unusual trapezoidal internal form. These dominant site conditions which create a complex, sculptural form and orientate its most open facade to the canal, while presenting a more solid elevation to the streets to the south. It is subtle and coherent, an addition to the city which brings out the best of

this previously unloved part of town. It undoubtedly provided the gateway statement that the planners sought and has an appropriate civic presence which feels like the missing piece of a complex urban jigsaw.

Its success is a compliment not only to Derwent and their architects Stiff + Trevillion, but also to the local planning authority which had provided the team with such a clear and ambitious brief of progressive mixed-use development targets. People comment today that it feels as if it has been there forever—the entirety of Derwent's Portobello Dock has quickly meshed with its surroundings to become an integral part of the familiar urban scene, modern yet referential.

The use of white StoRender, which Stiff + Trevillion had first used for Siemens at Roke Manor, became a favourite motif for their projects. Used here it quite clearly references the white architecture of nearby Kensal House. StoRender stays bright for years due to its unique chemical composition, which means it ages well. The development will therefore undoubtedly prove to be as timeless as its older cousin across the other side of Kensal Rise. However, the treatment also has deeper significance in the overall plan of the development. In a city which for a significant part of the year is dark and overcast, its sparkling whiteness stands out like a beacon of optimism in the gloom, symbolically reflecting light back into the surrounding streets like some great solar mirror and raising the spirits of the surrounding community. In short it represents the use of architecture as a symbol for a bright new future, the beginning of an opportunity to kick-start urban regeneration.

THE NEXT BIG FINANCIAL CRASH

Portobello Dock was Stiff + Trevillion's largest single London development to date and an unqualified success both on an urban design level and as a development. Completed in 2007, the residential element was sold quickly. Tom Dixon decided to move his studio to the west of London, took over the White Building, and set up the Dock Kitchen restaurant alongside the canal basin, adding an important cultural dimension.

The young drinks company innocent, took the entire 25,000 square feet at Canal Building and immediately commissioned Stiff + Trevillion to undertake the fit-out works. Led by Dan Campbell, the new headquarters needed to reinforce the distinctive work culture which innocent had established at its previous premises. The design challenge was to find a way of transferring the feel of the original workspace—arranged over just two storeys and permitting horizontal communication—to a six-storey building. The architects achieved this by removing part of the first floor and opening up a double-height communal space as an internal hang-out 'piazza', furnished with picnic booths, table football and an archetypal British telephone box, with funky contemporary graphics along Stüssy lines. The space was large enough for the entire company to gather together, an important corporate bonding event which happens at least

ABOVE The London Design Festival at Portobello Dock, organised by Tom Dixon in 2010.

OPPOSITE Portobello Dock viewed from the Canal Building, showing the upper entrance portico and the modulated interior lighting.

TOP AND BOTTOM The canal building reception, fair-faced shuttered concrete contrasts with the white piano lacquer of the desk and stair.

OPPOSITE TOP The canal building from Kensal Rise Cemetery with Trellick Tower in the distance.

OPPOSITE BOTTOM View of the Canal Building from one of the 'loft' penthouses and Portobello Lofts from Regent's Canal.

once a week. The design of the space was open, democratic and intended to keep the employees close to each other to retain the creative buzz, an essential part of the brand's continued evolution and socially aware identity. Today, all of innocent is now contained within the cool enclosure of Stiff + Trevillion's fantastic space, which acts as a neutral backdrop, both outside and inside, to the city and the lives of those who use it. In a letter sent by Richard Reed, one of the three founders of innocent, he stated:

I just wanted to say we absolutely love our new home.... I think it is a combination of two things: firstly, the original architecture—the sense of space, light and air means it's a wonderful building to be in. Secondly, the refit works—the chillout acts as a great hub for community, people can work at their desks and even stairs act as a source of energy and a place to socialise.... Nice one Stiff + Trevillion.[6]

Stiff + Trevillion went from strength to strength and in 2006 the partners decided to move premises again. This time it was further downstream from Portobello Dock to 4,500 square feet of office space beside the canal in the shadow of Erno Goldfinger's iconic Trellick Tower. It was David Rosen who alerted them to the vacant property, an old warehouse converted by Ben Kelly for PR consultant Lynn Franks (famously caricatured as Eddie in the hit TV show *Absolutely Fabulous*). Adopting some of the innocent working principles, albeit re-interpreted in the context of a design studio, here at last everyone was contained on a single floor. There were meeting rooms and chill-out areas too, plus an entrance full of posters and cut-outs from the latest design magazines and littered with employees bicycles. It is cool, relaxed and communal—very much in the spirit of Mike's first office experiences as a trainee at David Rock's Dryden Street studio way back in the 1970s.

By 2008 the company had a steady flow of interesting, high-end work coming in. Richard Cook was expertly advising them and they had decided that a new, more up-to-date brochure promoting the work of the practice was now required. Much had changed in the space of five years since the previous book was launched and this time they went for a more substantial piece, the so-called "black book", again designed by Wordsearch. It largely comprised of beautifully shot photographs showcasing the best buildings Stiff + Trevillion had done over the past 20 years (which was generally the work of architectural photographer Killian O'Sullivan, with whom they had developed a clear understanding of what was required for each commission). The book was like an old fashioned portfolio in manageable form, elegantly formulated and presented. Some of their younger colleagues might have been excused for asking why, in this age of online PR, the partners still insisted on producing such an expensive vehicle for promotion—it seemed rather old fashioned to some. But Mike and Andy simply felt that there is something tangible about a book—like a building—you can hold it, feel it, keep it, even smell it. It is present and resonates in a way that the mostly ephemeral electronic publications can't hope to match. Plus if it gets one

new job in it has paid for itself. Enigmatically enclosed in high-quality, textured black binding, this was something they could leave with clients after an important pitch meeting, an intriguing little piece of Stiff + Trevillion memorabilia that could be handled, examined and weighed, an *aide memoire* for prospective clients to remind them of the body of outstanding work the practice had carried out during its history.

In the context of the global economy, the compilation of the extravagant "black book" came at a strange time in the story of the firm. Stiff + Trevillion had looked at a few other developments with Richard Cook since the success of Latimer Road and as their friendship blossomed they considered doing a joint venture. Mike spotted an interesting site for sale in Latimer Road not far from the Designers Guild which seemed like a suitable vehicle for the project. Planning was approved and initially they intended to develop it themselves and use part of the building as their own offices as an ongoing investment. However, when they tested the market they found that although there was little appetite for rentals, there was a lot of interest in purchasing it. The musician Damon Albarn, who lived locally, agreed to buy it and retained Stiff + Trevillion to do the conversion for him. Fortunate caution perhaps before the storm that was to follow.

ABOVE innocent HQ, fit-out
works with meeting rooms
and the library, 2011.

OPPOSITE innocent open-plan
office space.

On 15 September 2008, the financial services firm Lehman Brothers filed for Chapter 11 bankruptcy protection in the USA, the largest suit in corporate history with $600 billion of exposure. A significant portion of this had been invested in the sub-prime mortgage market in the United States. This event had a domino effect on the global economy, with the numerous hedge funds that relied on Lehman's having to de-leverage overnight. Banks across the world suffered from the flight of the investors, including the London based Royal Bank of Scotland which had become the fifth largest bank in the world posting an operating profit of £10.3 billion in 2007. By September 2008 it was about to go bust when the British government stepped in with a massive investment of tax payers' money to cover its potential losses of £30 billion.

What has been described as a colossal failure of common sense, was within a week threatening to become the biggest economic depression in history. Even safe businesses like Stiff + Trevillion were for a brief time under real threat as developers ran for cover and banks panicked—anyone that was involved in property was at risk.

Despite the fact that they now had only a small, rarely used overdraft, the bank called the partners in for monthly meetings. Their accountant panicked them too and they started to have visions of 1990. They considered laying off some of their staff to weather the predicted storm. Fortunately Richard Cook stepped in. He took a long hard look at the list of the practice's creditors and concluded that if all that was owed was paid, there was not going to be a problem. In fact the fee forecasting procedures Cook and Trevillion had put in place earlier now stood them in good stead, demonstrating that the business was in fine shape for the next six months at least, even in the event of them earning no further income during that time—an unlikely scenario they believed. The partners hunkered down and waited. Christmas 2008 was an anxious time but as it gave way to the New Year debts were quickly settled and work continued to come in. Despite being in the midst of yet another recession, the "black book" was compiled, published and sent out and began to work its magic. They were weathering the storm effortlessly.

AFTER 2008 AND THE PLANNING GAME

Post-Lehman Brothers, many similar-sized practices involved in public sector commissions—schools, hospitals, social housing, cultural projects generally—contracted significantly and lost many of their most prized assets, their best employees. Sadly for those who had worked so hard to build these practices up, some closed down forever. What the recession did was to sort the wheat from the chaff, the strong from the weak. If a developer was struggling before the crash in September 2008, they would almost certainly have been sent over the edge by skittish banks calling in their borrowings. Significantly those involved in private developments at the upper end of the spectrum fared much better. What the recession provided was very low interest rates and a number of enforced sales by those developers who were in trouble. This in turn promoted a degree of rationalisation within the industry which, one could argue, was no bad thing.

There was also the added benefit of a free-floating, controllable currency—Sterling (Gordon Brown had prevented Tony Blair from taking the UK into the Euro-zone)—which meant that the pound could devalue itself freely against the euro and other world currencies. This devaluation attracted investors from other countries to invest in the London property market at a reduced premium. This had a significant effect on higher end property prices as investors from Russia, Germany, France, China (Hong Kong in particular), even Australia and the USA, piled their money into residential property. All of this was good news for Stiff + Trevillion as it encouraged new developments for their residential sector.

Their determination throughout the practice's evolution to resist at all costs the blandishments of public sector commissions had now finally been justified. They had become known as private sector architects and this gave them a significant edge, in terms of their networks and their knowledge, over more generalist practices of a similar size. Within that framework they had carved out for themselves three distinct design sectors, they weathered the storm and then thrived. They had taken to heart Richard Cook's advice in 2008 "Get the money in and sit tight." This proved to be sound counsel—over the five years since the cataclysmic events of 2008 Stiff + Trevillion's turnover has doubled and the practice has effectively also doubled in terms of employees.

Arguably the downside of the influx of foreign money flooding the London property market is that it is mostly speculative investment supporting some distant property portfolio in another continent. Properties are frequently held as empty residential investments consequently stifling the growth of the small shops, businesses and affordable housing in the surrounding area which provide the life-blood of any city. The vibrancy which derives from a thriving amalgam of mixed users—families, singletons, retailers and professionals—and which fuels the virtuous circle of the traditional walking city, risks being diluted as the city centre becomes stratified and lifeless, just as the City of London lost its residential component in the 1950s to end up devoid of life in the evenings and at weekends. As we write there are a number of stories in the press about high-end residential streets and squares in Kensington and Chelsea which have suffered this fate and can now count only one or two resident families in situ. Of an evening the area is largely in darkness, silent and dead, a reality which flies in the face of everything Stiff + Trevillion themselves enjoy and value about urban life.

For architects such as Mike, Richard and Andy there is always an ethical dimension to their work, in their hearts they believe in the common good, public space for the use of people of all types, facilitating adjacent mixed uses and blended communities. However Stiff also believes that this influx of wealthy investors at the higher end of the market does allow architects to build to better budgets which in turn improves the overall quality of these locations. This eventually filters down to the community end of the market, with higher quality arts buildings, schools, hospitals and much improved design of affordable housing.

Negotiating planning permissions is one of the few skills an architect still controls on a project. (Stiff believes that the profession has largely handed over control of contract management and masterplanning in recent years). On more complex schemes the use of planning consultants is now a prerequisite because the system has become almost Kafkaesque in its absurd complexity. Inevitably, as developers get smarter the system spins further webs of bureaucracy to restrain them. Urban planning is clearly very important but the UK legislation now governing it is so complex it cannot adapt quickly enough to the market as it evolves. A good example of this is in the City of Westminster where the local authority has always striven to encourage the development of more homes. This is not a bad policy in itself but the regulations state that any application for office space needs to provide an equivalent amount of residential, a proportion of which needs to be affordable housing. This often makes it extremely difficult to make the development case stack-up where land and property values are sky high. As well as this, some authorities are encouraging office-to-residential conversions. Not surprisingly, in areas where residential values are three times that of office rentals, developers are jumping over each other to convert offices into luxury homes. This market shift has been relatively swift—it seems that planning policy cannot adapt quickly enough to address the issues that global capitalism is throwing up.

While there is undoubtedly a certain institutional lethargy in tackling the bigger picture, at a more granular level this situation leads to meddling in detailed issues and design in particular. For architects and their developers seeking to build modern (as opposed to vernacular) or iconic expressive buildings in tightly constrained conservation areas, the planning process can be incredibly frustrating. All too often it will seem like a personal battle between two competing ideologies, the 'reactionary planners' pitted against the far-sighted 'visionary architect', depending on your point of view.

When Stiff + Trevillion started practising in the early 1980s the planning process was to some degree like this, often confrontational, and the two men had consequently come to see urban planners as the enemies of good design and creative thinking. Today the planning process in central London can be much more collaborative. Stiff + Trevillion work with planning consultants such as Gerald Eve, Turley Associates and DP9, most of whom have worked in local authorities previously and have an intimate working knowledge of the byzantine machinations of the system. PR consultants organise the public exhibitions of the proposals to meet consultation requirements and organise presentations to ward councillors. It is all highly political and the power wielded at council level when determining an application may hinge on the proximity of the next council election. At the same time this rich but often frustrating process has in the better boroughs created a more productive relationship between developers, their architects and the design officers in the planning teams.

In 2008 the Royal Borough of Kensington and Chelsea, under the control of Councillor Daniel Moylan, established an Architectural Appraisal Panel (AAP) to improve quality and to provide informed guidance and advice to architects new to the borough wishing to make fresh planning applications on behalf of their clients. A number of high profile architects including David Chipperfield, Will Alsop, John McAslan and Michael Squire were invited to provide the required insights needed when working within this well-heeled locality and Mike Stiff was also wooed. As a member of the RBKC AAP, Mike can now see the way the system works from a different angle, and this has definitely helped him to understand the issues and frustrations the planners have to deal with.

In all this, a good architect who understands the system will find that effective liaison with planners is one of the principle skills that any client will look for. Sometimes this makes it hard for younger practices to break into the system and build in sensitive locations and it is another reason why inspired developers are invaluable to the architect. Derwent London have really helped firms like Squire and Partners, John McAslan, AHMM and Duggan Morris to name only a few, by getting them into the crucial central London market, but this has taken considerable time and a robust determination on all sides. For architects like Stiff + Trevillion success has not come overnight, it has come after hard work and a long-term commitment to the commercial market.

Perhaps more than ever, younger practices have to understand how the planning system works and not be afraid to seek the advice and support of other professionals and consultants in this regard. The presentation skills that are developed at university via the traditional crit system come into their own at public consultations, design reviews and planning meetings. The best local authority planners and the time-consuming process that is modern town planning can, in the hands of a capable architect and a good developer, produce better results. It all comes down to team work.

CADOGAN—A BREAK THROUGH COMMISSION

For businesses which develop in a traditional way, growing organically over decades in step with the knowledge and experience amassed by their owners, there comes a point when something really significant changes and there is a sense of having reached and successfully hurdled the final big fence on the course. For some manufacturing businesses this might be a critical piece of technology which has put that business ahead of its competitors, in the case of architectural practices this moment usually comes after a successful pitch, there can be a sense of scale, significance and responsibility not previously experienced.

Such a moment happened to the practice of Stiff + Trevillion in October 2009. The pitch was for a new office and retail development of 13,530 square metres, a substantial project on one of the most prestigious boulevards in London, with a 60-metre frontage at the southern end of Sloane Street, near Sloane Square.

Initially they had been faintly surprised to be included on the shortlist for a limited competition to develop the site. The invitation came in a letter which was almost overlooked in their post box. All incoming mail was open at the front of the office available for everyone to see (a lesson from the Rock Townsend days). A couple of days later Mike had a look at the site and was stunned, this was potentially a very big job for the practice.

Stiff + Trevillion were determined to make the most of what they saw as a privilege, albeit a potentially expensive one if unsuccessful, but the project would undoubtedly be a positive challenge for the practice. They were up against larger more established firms used to working with Cadogan, Paul Davis & Partners, Squire and Partners amongst others. However they liked the urban and contextual questions posed by the site, and committed a significant level of resource to the pitch with a design team led by Mike and Daniel Campbell. However, the development process was opened-up to wider scrutiny within the office, with open reviews, pin-ups and design discussions with anyone who had the time and the motivation to get involved. Within the office it was a fully interactive process. The pitch alone was to last nine months from beginning to end.

The proposals would involve the demolition of two outdated 1960s office and retail buildings, both of course originally built by the Estate. The brief was consistent and clear, the new buildings needed to be grade A office space, with top quality retail that would need to inform the street level areas. Planning consultants Gerald Eve would guide the scheme through the planning process, and they would have a say in the final selection process too. As all of the practices were fully conversant with the Royal Borough of Kensington and Chelsea's planning processes, it seemed that it would constitute a fairly level playing-field. Mike felt confident that success would hinge on design quality and also to some degree on the personalities of those involved. He was also very aware that as a smaller design focused practice they were in the pitch as outsiders.

Between January and April 2009 they put in a huge amount of work. The preliminary pitch comprised a 120-page document which was comprehensive with a design based around the creation of a new public courtyard to the rear of the scheme that allowed the basement of the Sloane Street retail units to be opened to fresh air and natural light, in the style of Corso Como in Milan. This strategy was intended to double the area of top-grade retail, a clever and well remembered urban strategy. A restaurant and smaller artisan shops were intended to invigorate the courtyard and create a new mixed-use destination in this part of the city.

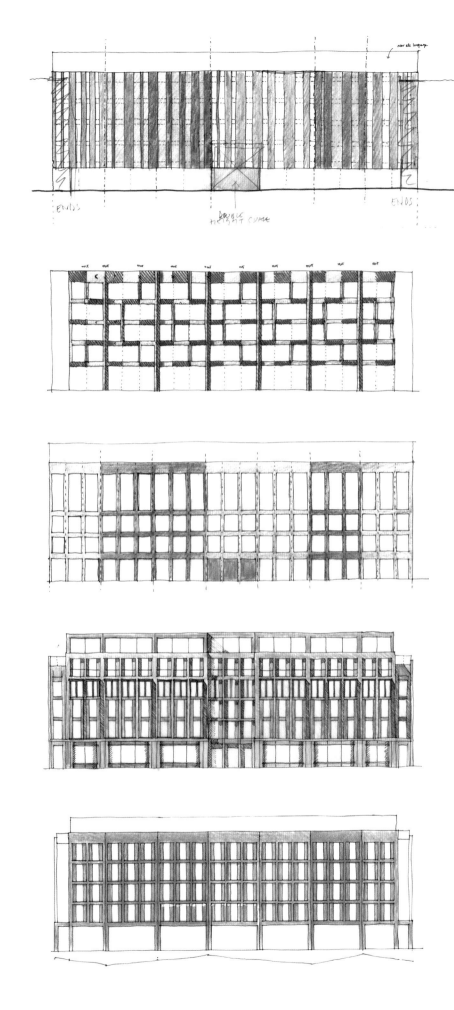

197

OPPOSITE 127–135 Sloane Street, the two original 1960s buildings.

RIGHT Elevational development sketches of the principle Sloane Street facade, drawn by Sean Crummey.

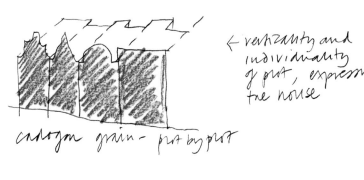

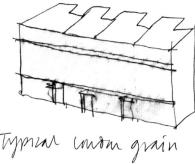

↚ verticality and individuality of plot, expressing the house

cadogan grain - plot by plot

↚ horizontality and homogeneity of terrace. small plots made to look like a big building or palace

Typical london grain

ABOVE LEFT Corso Como Milan, views of the restaurant courtyard, which was an important reference during the Cadogan pitch enabling them to communicate their intentions for a similar courtyard treatment at the rear of the Sloane Street development, (due to be completed 2016).

ABOVE RIGHT AND OPPOSITE
Cadogan Estate. Mike Stiff sketch analysis of the historical context at pitch stage.

For the main building facing onto Sloane Street, an understanding of the *genius loci* of the estate's historical buildings mostly from the Victorian era, is clear in the choice of materials for the proposed new facade. It uses red Scottish sandstone, which recognises the need for a grand urban scale along this important street. The western elevation, courtyard and mews structures at the rear revert to a version of lower-grade stock bricks, which is an interpretation of the historical norm for this type of building which makes-up the bulk of the Cadogan Estate's properties. It has a sense of ordered spatial hierarchy, with historicist references which are nevertheless fresh and modern. To be successful it needed to have a real presence but in an understated conservative form.

After three months and a further presentation the shortlist was reduced to two practices, Stiff + Trevillion and Squire and Partners. References were taken, relevant projects were visited and further interviews and revised design studies were presented. Cadogan were cautious, this was a big scheme in the heart of the estate, whatever they built would be there for a long time. According to Mike Stiff, the Great Estates are different to many developers in that they are "stewards", they must think long term, a new building may be there for at least four generations, perhaps longer if it has the appropriate staying power. Cadogan is a family business which is run by property professionals. They can't afford to make mistakes and they allow time for the correct decision to emerge.

For the final presentations, they needed to step things up a gear. They carved out a team which comprised Dan Campbell, Sean Crummey, Emily

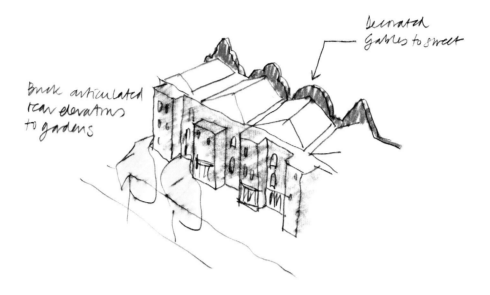

Cadogan Estate Front and Back.

Decorated Gables to street

Brick articulated rear elevations to gardens

Lawley, Selvei Al-Assadi and David Kahn with Stiff and Trevillion always involved. Crummey was the lead designer, someone who has worked for Stiff + Trevillion from the earliest days, an architect of great skill and precision. They needed long hours and commitment for the final push. As an office they work hard and play hard (when the time is right). They have never encouraged the all night work ethic, common in many architectural practices when there is an important deadline looming. Stiff recalls his own trainee days at Chapman Taylor, when he had been in the office working late one night, Bob Chapman told him in no uncertain terms that "if the job was being run properly, you would not be working at this late hour. It is not being resourced if it can't be done in normal office hours". This recommendation has remained with Mike ever since, however sometimes 'needs must'.

For the final interview, they had the initial copy of the "black book" ready which was handed to Hugh Seaborn. Mike likes to think that it helped. The presentation included printed documents, card models and Stiff's drawings of facade studies, where the greatest design changes had occurred between this and the successful scheme presented at the interim interview. Previously they had shown the scheme dressed in white stone, the change to red sandstone was risky, it is a material which is difficult to work and is often not used well in London. However, it obviously felt right from a contextual position and explained their thinking cogently. They fielded many other questions during the hour-long interview, a number of which focused on the firm's lack of previous experience at this scale of operation (it would be their largest commission in London

to date, by far). They realised that for Cadogan, their appointment would be a leap of faith, and tried to reassure the interview panel that as new clients, for a commission of this importance, they would receive partner involvement at all stages of the design and build phase. However, they felt reasonably confident. If they failed, it would not be due to lack of commitment. They knew that their scheme was strong.

On the way back to the office after the final presentation, Mike and Dan went for a quick lunch at the Anglesea Arms in South Kensington to wind-down. They were both exhausted, experiencing that typical sense of anti-climax, when you have seemingly run the race, put in all the training and made the final explosive effort fuelled by pure adrenalin to reach the winning tape, but you still do not know if you have won or come second. It was now a waiting game, and there was lots more to do which was not about Cadogan. Even if they did not win the commission on this occasion, things were looking good for Stiff + Trevillion.

Mike Stiff heard they had won as he was driving up to Lincoln to open the Making History exhibition for the Society of Antiquaries. The news filled him with a sense of pride and relief—this was it, a once-in-a-lifetime opportunity. It takes many years and does not happen often in an architect's career, but moments like this make the years of slog and endeavour worthwhile. After crossing the Humber Bridge he pulled into a lay-by and telephoned his wife and the office to share the news. Whilst many other practices were still struggling in the shadow of the financial melt-down, for Stiff + Trevillion 2009 had been a very good year.

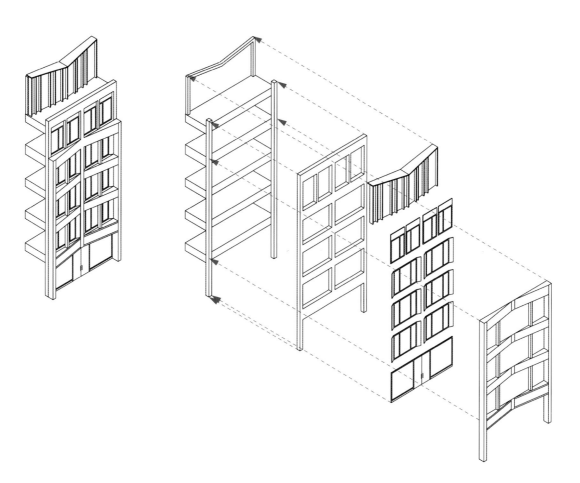

Inevitably their thoughts and actions moved on to the next phase, the planning application. Architecture is always full of so many variables which inevitably have knock-on effects, to the extent that almost until the very day the building is complete and handed-over, a spirit of change and adaptation is necessary. The requirement to constantly refine and adjust the design on numerous different levels, albeit with the use of complex analytical software and three-dimensional modelling. However it is not product design, where you can test full-scale mock-ups whilst changes are still being implemented. In architecture it is not possible, so rather like a very complex version of Rubik's Cube, a great many elements of the design will be in flux, to the last minute, pushing and pulling each other, forcing change on other aspects of the design. Part of the skill is to understand the aspects of the equation which are not negotiable and then to know when to stop changing and experimenting. The initial concept needs to be strong and robust, a nonnegotiable thesis to which everyone in the team is signed-up to.

The planning process was a lengthy one, but the team had time (vacant possession would not be possible until the end of 2012). This period was well spent, it would be a big building within a conservation area in close proximity to other listed buildings to which some deference would be required. Ultimately the design was supported by the planners and it developed further with their input following a number of presentations to the AAP.[7] The entire process was, Mike believes, constructive. Finally, in December 2011 planning permission was granted. Michael Squire was the first to congratulate them, he is, Mike believes, a true gentleman, an

exceptionally talented and visionary architect who is barely recognised within the rarified echelons of the so-called architectural *cognoscenti*.

To the extent that the civic presence and urban scale of the commission were on the level of Mike and Andy's earliest ambitions, Stiff + Trevillion had finally arrived.

THE PLANNING DOCUMENT AND 10–4 PENTONVILLE ROAD

The Cadogan Design and Access Statement, a document prepared for the Planning Application and Conservation Area consent, summarises Stiff + Trevillion's strategy for this particular project. It is a masterpiece of brevity and precision. It is also charming and to some degree romantic in its pragmatic business-like manner, describing the scheme in shorthand, summarising their intentions for the client's benefit as well as making definitive commitments about the architectural quality needed to meet the planning committee's exacting standards. It is a distinctive proposal which is totally 'Stiff + Trevillion', combining critically important historicist and contextual rigour with ruthless commercial discipline. It engages their key design skills and is accessible avoiding the impenetrable architect-speak so common to this type of specialist documentation. It is almost joyful in its spirit, one can easily understand why the client would have given them the commission based on this articulate statement of intent.

The art of doing urban architecture is often contradictory, the ability to hold two opposing ideas in your head at the same time is necessary, for example. It's simple but it's also complex. However, of equal importance the report illustrates that crucial attribute, the capacity to communicate succinctly without losing passion. Deprived of that the client can have little confidence. Important historical precedents are cited, both of the past and of the present. For example, in trying to describe their idea for a new public space at the rear of the scheme, they illustrate archetypal urban courtyards from Corso Como in Milan to Heddon Street in Soho as precedents. The analysis includes a facade bay study of the archetypal Chelsea facade treatment from the Victorian and Edwardian eras of local mansion block developments. This is shown as

ABOVE The Sloane Street elevation.

OPPOSITE Plan of the landscaped courtyard to the rear of the development, drawn by Townshend Landscape Architects.

a deconstructed assembly of elements, drawn in axonometric from back to front, starting with the main body of the building, a solid, dense red brick wall, through to the 'add-on' brick bays, towers and porticoes, the second layer. They in turn lead to a particular treatment for the fenestration and reveals, sometimes finished with decorative dressed stonework, or simply painted white, this comprises the third layer. These fascia treatments and over panels "add depth, layering, privacy and shading".

The new facade treatment takes its cue from the logical build-up of this particularly important precedent, which is also explained in terms of its horizontal and vertical hierarchy from the base "which is larger in scale and deeper, changing as it goes up to the fifth floor office level, which is a much lighter freer structure". The new facade is of its time and distinctive but also incorporates two different grid systems which reflects the repetitive modulation of the adjacent terraces along Sloane Street. Ultimately it is a celebration of historical continuity, a recognition that the city is better when the majority of its building stock fits together harmoniously with its neighbouring buildings. In other words, it does not need to be a statement of individuality.

This detailed and articulate urban analysis harks back to their student training where they learned to use historical references as a short-hand way to illustrate and justify their design strategies.

It's like... Pallazo Massimo alle Colonne in Rome, adopting a grand, modern, unifying facade to the front, in an inventive Mannerist style, whilst at the rear, it merely incorporates and improves the existing lower scale elements....

(they might have stated during important presentations.) Thus, the more you know about traditionally orientated cities, throughout the world, the easier it is to describe your thinking using this informed referencing system, and the more erudite you will appear. It encapsulates the essential nature of Stiff + Trevillion's approach to architecture which has hardly erred over the 30 odd years since they learnt to work this way at the Poly.

This is not exclusive, other influences have come into play over the intervening years, as the partners have constantly enriched their knowledge with study and work trips abroad and surrounded themselves with interesting people, both their employees and their ever changing flow of social and business acquaintances. As frequently stated in this text, in a pluralistic age, values which are contemporary and reflect the *zeitgeist* are fundamental. Often as a direct result of their diverse range of commissions, and the way in which historical precedents are built into their DNA, these influences have been implanted subconsciously.

The project for the Cadogan Estate may come to be seen as the most pivotal job of recent years for Stiff + Trevillion. Not only is it the biggest job the office had yet undertaken, it is also an architecturally significant building on a prime site in London, which will form part of the backdrop to millions of lives in the future. It is an onerous responsibility but also places the usual logistical decisions onto Mike, Andy, Richard and Dan. Once the outcome of the planning process was clear Stiff + Trevillion began to assemble the right team to build it, which is not necessarily the same as the design team. Unusually it was going to be tendered traditionally with a Bill of Quantities, which meant that every nut and bolt needed to be identified and specified to form the watertight documents which were to be sent out for competitive tenders. This poses its own challenges, it means that the architect needs to be able to design and co-ordinate every aspect of the project with nothing left to chance or to a contractor's whim. A team would need to be assembled to do this, with the appropriate forensic minds in charge, leading from the front.

The core of the delivery team would be Sean Crummey, who had joined Stiff + Trevillion from David Richmond Architects in 2000, Nick Delo, a designer Mike Stiff had worked with on the Royal Academy exhibitions and David Kahn an architect with exceptional management and technical expertise whom Stiff had met when they worked together on the Royal Lancaster Hotel project (they had been commissioned to fit-out the restaurant by architect and former tutor from the Poly days, Eric Parry). Kahn had learnt much about stone detailing whilst at Eric Parry Architects, an important skill since Sloane Street was to be clad in Scottish sandstone. Other new members to the practice were subsequently brought in each for their own particular technical skills. If anything was lacking in terms of expertise, it was addressed as the practice geared-up.

The Cadogan design team would peak at around ten people during the production of the technical drawings and specifications. Students can learn the ropes on jobs like this, as well as contributing to the design process through model-making and computer modelling. They too have an important contribution to make. Stiff + Trevillion had learned to their cost when they had built the Treptow project with Doug Clelland 20 years before, that you can't skimp on manpower when you are commissioned to build a big new building, and particular skills have to be brought-in to ensure complex projects of this type are not sold short.

Dan Campbell has worked alongside Mike on the development of Cadogan almost since its inception. An equity partner in the practice since 2004, he has become a key member of the team, bringing to the mix a younger dimension, presenting a less guarded more open face than the older partners can muster. Some clients find this reassuring, for example Richard Reed, the founder of the youthful and appropriately named innocent brand, is the same age as Dan; this means that in terms of the values and culture which informed their early years, they are aligned, they speak a similar language. As Mike, Andy and Richard moved into their 50s, this felt like the beginnings of the next generation of the practice, new faces began to assume greater responsibility, with the status to match. The main developer clients still wanted Mike, the smooth running of the office and critical crisis management strategies were still handled by Andy, but with Dan, the next generation seemed to be emerging. This was important for the clients, they could see that the practice was moving forward there was now a sense of continuity about the business, which is reassuring.

Dan was brought up in rural Derbyshire, he won a scholarship to Giggleswick School, a private boarding school in the Yorkshire Dales. There, in addition to his academic work, he learnt to be well organised and assertive in his dealings with people. At school, having combined the arts with the sciences, he was pleasantly surprised to hear that the school's careers profile at the age of 16 was directing him towards architecture. Even in those early days it felt right, but it needed to be aspirational, a high energy varied working environment, and most importantly, it needed to be design led.

Mike Stiff had met Campbell at the Sheffield University School of Architecture, when he had been doing some studio teaching in diploma during the late 1990s. Stiff led a field study trip to Berlin, and subsequently presented some of their projects to the student group, illustrating the design-led orientation of the practice. Having worked for a number of architects in the Sheffield locality, Campbell had been largely disappointed with their approach to the business of commercial design, working on a couple of car showrooms and half understood school buildings, both typologies expressed in a lazy 'tin-shed' aesthetic were not where he wanted to be. Campbell was suitably impressed by the Stiff + Trevillion approach, where architecture always came first. In 1999, having completed the diploma, he asked to work at Stiff + Trevillion. From there the relationships flourished, and the practice has expanded significantly during the 15 years of Campbell's involvement. Dan became an equity partner in Stiff + Trevillion in 2004. This was no doubt a shrewd move by the three partners; not only did it inject some young blood, it also ensured that a highly-valued colleague would be a big part of the future development of the business.

As ever with Stiff + Trevillion, the friendship came first, the business commitment followed. For Campbell who never intended to live and work in London, it has come as something of a culture shock, however the ability to adapt to new circumstances is essential within the new global market place.

BUILDING IN LONDON

The work with Derwent London continued in Islington, when in 2009 they were invited to look at 10–4 Pentonville Road. The site comprised two unattractive brown tinted glass buildings of 1970s vintage, (originally designed by EPR, the practice Andy Trevillion had briefly and unhappily worked for in the early 1980s). The brief was to create a new single building of handsome civic proportions which would age well, a tried and tested Derwent strategy which aims at a long-term increase in value over time. In a prominent location almost at the top of the steep hill which leads from King's Cross up to the Angel Islington, it is a site which guards one of the main traffic arteries leaving central London for the east. To Mike it felt like another 'gateway' building, however the available budget was not that great.

Rather than demolish, this would be a fast-track refurbishment, on the basis of a radical upgrade to the point where it feels completely new. The dated facades were removed and the robust concrete frame of the original was retained. To increase floor space they bridged over Angel Mews, from the second floor level and extended at the rear of number 10. However the main event is the new street facade which is an elegant essay in well-mannered Palazzo building which adopts a similarly complex amalgam of vertical and horizontal elements to Sloane Street, only this time formed out of a single unifying construction material, Danish Petersen bricks, a rich mix of slimly elongated white, grey and charcoal-fired units all bonded with lime mortar (which means that movement joints are eliminated giving the whole a much more authentic appearance, basically doing what brick walls should do, simply supporting their own weight). The salt and pepper effect both stands out against its neighbours, the proportions are similar to the neighbouring Georgian terraces, it fits-in. Again with a subtle sleight of hand, the architects having created a structure which is obviously modern but will feel like it has been there for generations in years to come.

They have repeated the Derwent formula in the new paired entrance areas, one either side of the mews service entrance, each has a simple Mies van der Rohe inspired cantilevered canopy which signals "entrance". Inside each new reception area there is a direct reference to the famous

10–4 Pentonville Road, showing
the junction between adjacent
listed stone building and the new
brick facade, 2012.

ABOVE 10–4 Pentonville Road,
looking north-east.

OPPOSITE 10–4 Pentonville
Road, facade detail.

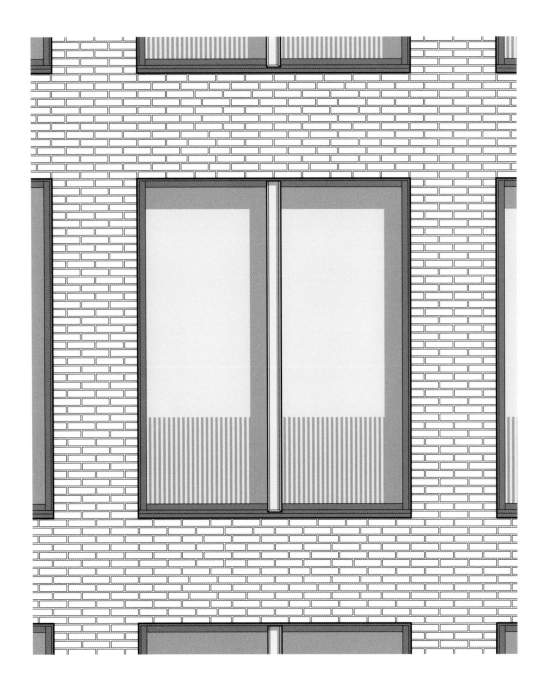

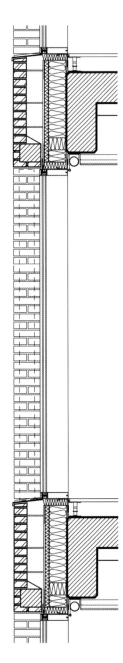

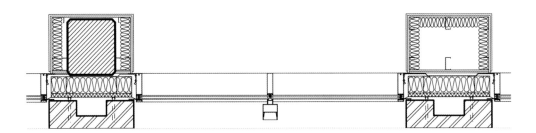

The brickwork at Pentonville was designed using lime mortar, which negates the requirement for unsightly movement joints. Part elevation, section and plan of a typical bay detail, 10–4 Pentonville Road.

TOP The anodised aluminium mullions reinterpret the wite painted reveals of the Georgian buildings.

BOTTOM Typical Georgian terrace in Islington showing how the white painted reveals and classically derived proportions influenced the new building, a modern take on a classical facade.

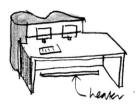

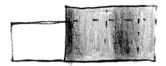

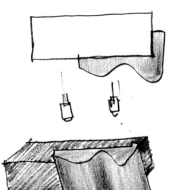

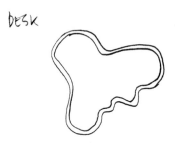

DESK

Scandinavian designer of the high Modern Movement, Alvar Aalto, with a reception desk which is clearly inspired by his Savoy vase design. With the use of robust clean materials, including polished concrete floors and timber panelling, this interior is built to last, creating the type of space within which you would feel comfortable each time you turn-up for work. It raises the spirits. Overall, Pentonville has contemporary architectural values yet at the same time, it refers to the local Georgian vernacular and to the Modern Movement in general, it has received widespread praise for its sense of grandeur and appropriateness, one of Stiff + Trevillion's preoccupations from the earliest days in practice

HOW TO ENSURE SUSTAINABILITY IN PRACTICE

There is a saying in Silicon Valley "ubiquity first, revenue later". This certainly applies for many architects who launch themselves into practice when they are hardly ready. Understandably so, having spent so many years at college, the itch to build becomes a fixation. It took Stiff + Trevillion a long time to change this attitude, the sense of relief and gratitude on winning a commission is always there, but it is a business, they have responsibilities and people to pay, fees are after all the lifeblood of the business, no profit equals no business. Discussing money at the outset of a project is a bit like agreeing a 'pre-nup' before marriage, very wise but distasteful.

Setting a fee which is a minimum has worked for Stiff + Trevillion with domestic clients, they are prepared to pay for quality, design and service. However, with commercial clients it is not as easy, there is cut throat fee bidding in the market place, and many clients will look at the fee rather than the architect. Thankfully this attitude is changing, the complexity of the planning process and the sophistication of the end user is driving design up the agenda. Blue-chip clients will always want a competitive fee,

but realise that it needs to be enough to allow the architect to resource the job. Quite simply, the fee needs to at least cover the overheads and staff time before it makes a profit to pay the directors. There is a rule of thumb that the practice has adopted, the fee must comprise one third overheads, one third staff costs and one third profit. The last third is the insurance policy, it is necessary not just to pay directors but also to cover unforeseen costs. An extended planning application negotiation for example.

Finding the correct balance of skills within each design team is critical, and sometimes opposites work well together. For example associate Ed Mullett joined a year after Dan Campbell, he also came from Sheffield University. After a year or two he became Mike Stiff's right hand man, together they have built Portobello, Pentonville, 1 Valentine Place, Queen's Apartments and currently they are working on Regent House for the Portman Estate. Mullett brings a good balance of design understanding and applied technical skill which is the linchpin of these complex projects. Whereas Mike is always focussing on the bigger picture, Mullett is fastidious, well organised and cool under fire, particularly when it comes to building "we have designed it this way, so that is the way it is going to be built". The relationship between the two architects is always dynamic, they are very different personalities, but perhaps this is what the business of creating buildings is all about. Sometimes Ed Mullett's forensic attention to detail can be annoying, we can deal with that in due course, Mike might say (implying that it's a detail), Mullett does not allow any level of ill-discipline to creep into the process, from the outset he is on the case. These are complementary

OPPOSITE LEFT Design development sketch for the reception desk.

OPPOSITE RIGHT An internal view of the main reception area.

LEFT 10–4 Pentonville Road, detail of the polished stainless 'cruciform' column supporting the main entrance canopy, 2010.

RIGHT Detail showing Petersen Brickwork with Bill Amberg leather bench seat inside the reception.

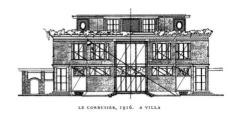

skill sets which insure against individual weaknesses in each and every member of the team.

The Woodfield Road offices were generous and would eventually accommodate the 40 or so in the business today. As ever, during this expansion of the practice, the partners sought first to find people through their network rather than through agencies. People not known to them would have to fit, there was no place for big egos or prima donnas at Stiff + Trevillion. The need to be part of the 'family' that the practice had become was the key priority. It is difficult to maintain the family idea as practices grow, they have states Andy, "worked hard to make sure that the studio remains social and essentially collegiate, conversations are struck up as and when they are needed, and the directors work in the same space so that the dialogue is always open, with certain obvious exceptions". Technical issues will be taken to Trevillion's table and even minor problems resolved in a spirit of informed cooperation. At their present size, the partners still know everyone, any larger they believe, it would cease to be a studio and it becomes an office. In an age of top down management speak, this ethos is important. The architecture business is not about predetermined theoretical systems of how to manage people, it is really all about the work, and how that can be achieved with the best results. If it ends up being about a studio of friends, where information exchange is constant, the practice will prosper.

For any practice the essential capital in networking and finding patronage is as important today as it was in the eighteenth and nineteenth centuries. Trying to succeed without the security of repeat business is impossible. Stiff + Trevillion believe that each new job is like the first job, even if it comes from a developer with whom they have previously worked. As a result of the sequence of great buildings they have produced for Derwent London over a sustained 15 year period, and the close personal relationship which has developed between Mike Stiff and Simon Silver, more commissions keep coming. Word gets around because like any professional group, developers have their own social and educational network, they all attend conferences together, case studies will be analysed, good ideas and architect recommendations will be handed around. Evidence of this can be seen in the ongoing enquiries the practice fields within their commercial sector, which largely come from within this developer's 'tribe'. Ask where they got Stiff + Trevillion's name from, and most developers may have read a favourable review and done some desktop analysis of the business, however the most critical decision will be based on discussions with one of their friends or colleagues in the developer's circle, can you work with these guys, are they flexible and adaptable, most importantly, is their work good from a design perspective and are they commercial, can they optimise the site's value?

So it was when a team approached them for help to optimise the value of their site at Valentine Place in London's Blackfriars Road. Stiff + Trevillion had worked with the owners previously, Michael Goldstein,

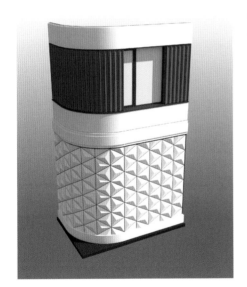

Howard Burkeman and Nic Byrom who had a long-standing planning consent for an office development. They asked Stiff + Trevillion to evaluate it with a view to enhancing its value. Initial thoughts around the planning consent were discussed with Southwark and it became clear that there was scope to add area if the quality of the design was improved. The usual fee had been agreed and the client suggested that there could be a pro-rata fee bonus for any additional area negotiated. For Stiff + Trevillion the site context suggested that there was scope for additional height on the corner of the plot, but the size of this new volume would only allow a single staircase and this would constrain the height because of means of escape requirements. Detailed negotiations proceeded and a smart scheme which resolved the access issues whist increasing the space was finally agreed and consent given in 2010. The development was completed in 2013 comprising seven floors of office space and a small retail unit on the ground, it has been designed to be multi-let, with a specification higher than might have normally been expected. The owners had been amongst the first to recognise the potential that would be unlocked by the arrival of the Jubilee line in the late 1990s. The increased volume at last made the development equation stack-up.

The building is similar in size to the Dock Building at Portobello, and they both share a similar core design with views out of the building into the lift lobby. Unusually for London they are both buildings with four elevations. But the budget was higher at Valentine Place, which has enabled them to specify a better quality facade. It is a very green building, achieving BREEAM "excellent".[7] By increasing the quality and the size of

the building, the team have brought an enhanced environment and more high quality jobs to this developing corner of inner London. The scheme encapsulates the value of good architecture and enlightened patronage.

Now sustainability is clearly an important issue for any new commercial development. When Mike and Andy, together with Doug Clelland, built Treptow in Berlin during the 1990s they were all surprised by the importance the German construction industry attached to green issues—at that time they were probably ten years ahead of the UK in that respect. It was only when the green agenda became political, and the developer's agents woke up to the idea that a building which consumes less energy and emits less carbon is good for the tenant's image, and for their employees, that these issues were taken seriously in the UK. Stiff + Trevillion avoided the first phase of 'show-off' green technology, with the use of Photo Voltaic panels as a sort of external 'look at me' decoration and similarly pointless wind turbines on the roof, architects have generally integrated low-carbon passive technology into their buildings in an elegant and efficient way. This has brought with it better insulation, improved glass specifications and intelligent management systems which does much more to save energy than any active technological devises will ever achieve.

COMMERCIAL RESIDENTIAL PROJECTS

In 2014 Stiff + Trevillion now have three large residential schemes with developers Alchemi, two of which are on site as we complete this chapter. Alchemi is a young London development company led by a dynamic husband and wife team. Charlie Baxter is the numbers man and his wife Laura Marino leads the creative side. Laura discovered Stiff + Trevillion by word of mouth and through the Stiff + Trevillion website. She initially visited the studio in January 2012, since then things have moved quickly.

OPPOSITE East elevation detail.

LEFT 1 Valentine Place, view of typical a office interior with a view out to the London Eye, 2013.

RIGHT 1 Valentine Place, the reception area uses recycled timber cladding on the walls with a backlit opal glass reception desk, a functional place that is full of character.

1 Valentine Place,
east elevation at dusk.

Two years later the team have consent for two of their schemes, which includes a prestigious location close to Parliament Square on Victoria Street. Both will be on site within two years of the first hello.

55 Victoria Street is a very exciting project in design terms. The site is positioned at a point where the direction of this important street changes slightly and the new building is intended to act as a natural focus for the street's directional axis, like the obelisks in Baroque Rome. As a result of their urban knowledge, Stiff + Trevillion immediately recognised that this would be the right place for a taller element, a marker that celebrates the city in its own subtle manner. The result is a 12-storey corner tower element, highly visible. The building further explores the brick aesthetic of Pentonville Road, using Peterson bricks in lime mortar. The apartments have generous floor to ceiling heights and access to landscaped gardens at several levels. It is a suitably exciting end-piece to this account.

MAKING RESIDENTIAL PAY

For Stiff + Trevillion the practice's private residential work had been something of a staple from the earliest days. A house will often be the first relatively substantial project for a young architectural practice, its initiation if you will, an essential component for a forward-looking design portfolio. If it occurs at a time when architects are keen, when they have the time to invest in what can be the most labour intensive, client-facing of commissions, a 'residential' can be an effective testing ground for new ideas. Ultimately if it photographs well and incorporates a couple of novel design moves, or uses innovative technology in some way, it may well be the kind of small project that an architectural journal will publish, and it can therefore potentially provide excellent PR. A look at the great and good of architecture shows us how even figures like Le Corbusier, Mies van der Rohe, Philip Johnson and Louis Kahn all started with residential projects early on in their careers—they revisited these in maturity. Even Foster and Rogers' initial joint practice, Team 4, built a house for Su Roger's parents in Cornwall. These small projects functioned for all these architects as prototypes for the kind of work they would go on to create in the later phases of their careers, the work for which they were to find worldwide fame and fortune.

According to Dan Campbell, a residential project is manageable and intense. "It's a brief everyone understands", he says.

It's firstly a home but it also carries with it romantic aspirations, sometimes about technology, full of labour-saving devices, the house of the future. Often it holds other more regressive ideas—the Englishman's home is his castle and all that. Whatever the client's ideas may be, for the architect residential has a bit of everything.

Whilst largely agreeing with Campbell's sentiments, Mike Stiff is more circumspect. It is also very difficult work which can be fraught

with conflict—arguments and misunderstandings come with the territory. Clients change their minds more often on residential projects, understandably as they will be living there for many years after the architect has disappeared. On one level a house has to function, like a machine, but on another a home is an intensely personal expression of a client's self, something which can turn designing and building it into an emotional roller coaster for all concerned. From a business point of view building one-off houses is time-consuming and not very profitable—as your overheads grow it is often difficult to finish the build without making a financial loss.

In view of these considerations, and given that their practice had now moved on to a much bigger stage, why did Stiff + Trevillion continue with the residential commissions after 2000? The partners remained convinced that continuing with a range of specialisms instead of concentrating solely on the commercial work, was one of their practice's strengths. They believed that in the past this strategy had proved fundamental in enabling them to weather periods of recession and continue to grow, allowing them to shift their focus from one type of commission to another as fortune dictated. Furthermore they all sensed that residential was the type of work which could be made to be profitable but they had not yet found exactly the right way of managing these projects. They now felt more practiced in this particular area of work and appreciated that there were certain elements of the build which you could not cheapen. They had received feedback over a number of years on earlier projects, which they then returned to fix if something went wrong or needed adapting. It was a costly after-sales service but it was also a form of research invaluable in helping them to see how they could improve.

Whereas in earlier decades they had undertaken residential projects almost anywhere, by 2008 they found that the residential work was happening closer to home, largely in the area of Kensington and Chelsea which was their home turf. To anyone asking around the dinner tables of W11 "Do you know a decent architect for my house?", Stiff + Trevillion's name would invariably be mentioned in the top three or four likeliest candidates for the job. Understandably so—these were commissions which were based, not just on their proven expertise in designing and then delivering the built product, but crucially on their local knowledge and the ability to negotiate and win difficult planning approvals. Furthermore, since completing Damon Albarn's studio, Mike had become good friends with the musician and this inevitably led to further commissions from Damon's friends and colleagues. As a result the practice have designed homes for Adele, Jamie Hewlett, Richard Russell and Norman Cook among others. Discretion is essential when dealing with 'public' figures, something that has paid off for the practice.

From 1997 the incoming 'New Labour' team got its hesitant government up and running and continued to reinforce and extend the free-market liberalisation of the Thatcher years with minimal scrutiny and oversight of the banks. Ultimately this would prove to have catastrophic economic

55 Victoria Street, London SW1, a 12-storey residential tower that has been modelled to address the long axis towards Victoria Station, (to be completed, 2015).

consequences, combining the banks' traditional high street roll with the speculative casino tendencies of the City brokers. But across the Western world everyone was doing the same—it was a new global economic craze which was fuelling cheap and easy borrowing with the particularly dangerous sub-prime lending in the USA enabling even the poorest, most insecurely employed people to get onto the housing ladder. To some it seemed like a new egalitarian age with property ownership at the lower end of the housing market pushing prices up right into the most expensive areas of central London. As sure as night follows day a housing bubble was developing, particularly in inner London, with seriously wealthy foreign investors from Russia, the USA and even China beginning to invest in London property. For Stiff + Trevillion the news was not bad and residential commissions were coming thick and fast, but they continued their policy of hedging these commissions with other kinds of work in case the sector fell flat for whatever reason.

By 2002, the economy was looking distinctly rosy. Prime Minister Tony Blair, together with his Chancellor Gordon Brown, was re-elected for another five-year term. The Tories under William Hague's youthful leadership came a distant second and most people now realised that the Tories were irrelevant—Blair and New Labour were on many

levels more Thatcherite than most Conservative candidates. "Cool Britannia" became for a brief summer the rallying call reflecting a period of increased pride in the culture of London, as celebrated in a 1996 *Newsweek* cover headlined "London Rules."[9]

Ordinary people were increasingly viewing their properties as investments at this time. An inherited Victorian pile, if located on a good street in the right borough (Westminster, Islington, Kensington and Chelsea in particular) could be redeveloped with huge basements dug-out of the gardens which could often double the square footage and the subsequent value. These sorts of commissions were not about interior design, this was heavy duty work for architects and their contractors. The ability to negotiate a successful planning permission became a skill which necessitated careful diplomacy and good urban design of the Stiff + Trevillion variety. All the coherent urban thinking around Rome and Tokyo was suddenly a high value currency within this burgeoning market. Stiff + Trevillion found an effective way of communicating their knowledge but the challenge remained—how to make it profitable?

Prior to 2009, they had taken each project on in its own terms, balancing the fee precariously against other factors such as the scope for publicity and good networking potential, often allowing time to run-away in their passion to get the design right. So much so that they often lost money on residential work, discovering at the end that the time spent far exceeded the fee earned. They always completed the job for the pre-agreed fee, it was a matter of honour, but it was clear that other more profitable areas such as office buildings were effectively keeping the studio afloat. It was a situation which they could not allow to continue. It had for too long been instinctive, lacking in scientific rigour. Now all resources had to be identified and set against the certainty of the financial case.

OPPOSITE Heathview House Putney, remodelled rear elevation.

ABOVE View of the living space at the Heathview House in Putney.

However, there was profit there to be taken if the business case could be clearly determined. Richard Cook convened a number of in-house seminars where the partners and the key players within the residential team were tasked to analyse all of the time spent, set against the cost of that time, with other overheads brought into the equation. They fed-in the time for pitching and winning commissions, partner's design time, all risks were defined and costed by way of sophisticated accounting software. What emerged was a much more credible analysis which demystified the whole thing; they were able to place quantifiable value on every part of the service even accounting for unsuccessful pitches within the base-line equation. Quickly a set of fail-safe processes were put in place and a path towards profitability was clearly defined.

What evolved was clear, for example there is a threshold of around £500,000 below which they would find it difficult to make the job pay, by extrapolation the fee needed to be a 'not less than' figure, which established the client's clear priorities in terms of the value the architect's expertise brought to the table. Any potential client which baulked at such up-front commercialism clearly did not get it. There was little scope for negotiation.

In 2005, Chris Eaton with a host of experience in the sector, joined Stiff + Trevillion, tasked to run the residential section of the practice, his skills and knowledge have brought rigour and discipline together with complimentary knowledge. This specialist application has transformed the management processes. The whole area has been systematised, it has become a highly transparent self-contained entity, with its own internal accountability. It is administered by a skilled specialist Associate Director who runs it almost like a practice within a practice. The results of this more rationalised approach has been that the quality and value of projects has increased, the jobs are bigger and as a consequence the contractors they employ are better and more skilful in their own right. A case of success breeding success. Consequently the fees are good and they make a profit. In hindsight, this much more systematic approach is a lesson in practice.

MAYFLY COTTAGE AND MORE PROFITABLE RESIDENTIAL PROJECTS

It is perhaps surprising that Stiff + Trevillion did not complete their first totally new residential project until 2011. Mayfly Cottage is a contemporary, rural house commissioned by friends of Mike and located near Romsey in Hampshire. Their first new-build commission, it stands as something of a Stiff + Trevillion landmark.

Stiff's initial concern was to find the aesthetic appropriate to this sensitive site, situated between a beautiful thirteenth century church and a handsome Victorian manor house, without resorting to historical pastiche. His preliminary site analysis suggested that the new building should adopt a shape derived from the local vernacular, with a form which was subservient to the existing landmark buildings. It should

Mayfly Cottage near Romsey in Hampshire, view of the new building in the context of the original Victorian manor house, 2012.

SOUTH ELEVATION

NORTH ELEVATION

ABOVE Mayfly Cottage, elevations to the north and south.

OPPOSITE St Andrew's Church Timsbury, twelfth century church tower, with Mayfly Cottage in the foreground.

appear, in typological terms, analogous to a kind of barn structure, low and demure, in local terms secondary but typical. One of the most prominent building features which struck him on first visiting the locality were the ostentatious Victorian chimney stacks of the manor house. Clearly these two ideas were prompts for a potential narrative around which he could construct the design.

The key strategic moves were therefore clear to the architect from the start. Firstly, its overall form would be low and rectangular, adopting a similar pitched roof arrangement to the other historical out-buildings around it. Immediately this led to the intimate spaces, bedrooms and bathrooms, being positioned beneath the pitched part of the roof on the first floor. This enabled the ground floor layout to be diametrically opposed, mostly open and fluid, a modern living/studio space. Secondly, there was the chimney, which as a gesture assumed larger-than-life proportions at the centre of the plan (rather than being positioned on an external gable-end as is traditional). It became the symbolic centre of the house, the core of hearth and home, and because it nestles within the centre of the plan it emits radiant heat from the most environmentally effective place. This also works well functionally because it is surrounded by accommodation, rather than being on an outside wall, and doesn't obscure any of the external views all the way round the building, which blurs the barriers between inside and out. To emphasise its important role it was painted white rather than being left in rustic brick. According to Stiff this makes it appear more Scandinavian and contemporary in spirit.

228

ABOVE View from the dining room to the garden with the inside-outside effect of the sleek glazed doors.

OPPOSITE Green oak frame with the white painted brick chimney breast.

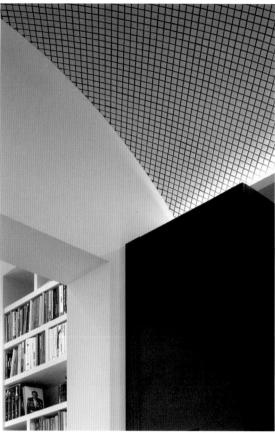

A green-oak frame was chosen with handmade bricks and roof tiles which were sourced locally. The client wanted the project to be very sustainable, so ground source heat pumps were installed in the garden. These exploit the natural heat trapped in the soil to provide hot water for the property without burning fossil fuels. The house was also fitted with photovoltaic panels to generate electricity and a rainwater harvesting system which helps to irrigate the garden. Stiff wanted the palette of materials to be limited to brick and timber cladding, in this case burned Siberian larch, to give the traditional barn-like form a modern twist. This is a renewably sourced timber which is also low in maintenance—once it has been burnt with a blow torch on site it develops an attractive weathered appearance and a hard rain screen type of finish which will last for 60 odd years. Zinc was used in areas requiring light-weight malleable finishes, such as the large dormer window and accentuated box gutters.

Inside the oak frame is visible—an element of satisfying functionality. Mike Stiff goes further, it is he states, "A thing of beauty in its own right, so we wanted its decorative presence to be visible in every room." Made of green oak with traditional dowel pegs, there are no screws or bolts used anywhere which means that the whole structure can move and settle. In tune with its natural setting it is a living, organic creature. Further accentuating this rustic feel the internal doors are ledged and braced oak, and most of the floors are also in oiled oak. The house has a reassuring and appropriate Arts and Crafts feel, reminiscent of the John Brandon-Jones inspired interiors Mike remembers from his second year at PCL. The owners have described their house in these terms:

ABOVE Notting Hill townhouse, Chepstow Villas, the open living room and detail of the tiled barrel vaulted ceiling to the kitchen, 2013.

OPPOSITE The kitchen and dining space, Chepstow Villas.

There's not one thing we wish we had designed differently. The house has a simple beauty without trying too hard, yet it is also contemporary. We love its framed views from so many aspects, so you constantly have the juxtaposition of the new house and old surroundings. It's an extremely easy house to live in, which we think is proof of good design.[10]

Mayfly Cottage is something of a one-off in terms of the residential commissions Stiff + Trevillion usually undertake. More typical perhaps is the conversion of a Victorian terraced house in Chepstow Crescent, in the residential heart of Notting Hill. It was in the shadowy months after the financial crash of September 2008 that Mette Hardie, a diminutive Danish mother of four, and her husband Norman, approached the practice. In the immediate aftermath of the crash, an over-leveraged developer had abandoned their uncompleted refurbishment and the flooded basement and structurally unsound party wall structures were now threatening to seriously destabilise the entire terrace. It was a gruesome vision of semi-dereliction in one of the wealthiest parts of west London.

The four storey mid-terrace was narrow and tall, reminiscent of the proportions of the buildings in central Amsterdam. It was the type of commission which combined heavy duty engineering work together with sensitive interior design. Stabilising the leaky structure came first and emergency remedial works made things safe within 24 hours as Stiff + Trevillion's site sign-board appeared reassuringly on the hoardings outside.

The emphasis on understanding the client's needs had now moved centre stage in Stiff + Trevillion's residential commissions. They found that Mette Hardie was well-informed and decisive and because she had a precise view about what she wanted and articulated things clearly, the work was a pleasure. They made a good team. Indeed the client's skill and knowledge about interiors chimed with Chris Eaton's to the extent that ultimately it was a wholly reciprocal relationship.

Although it was tall, and at least from the outside seemed capacious, in reality the interior of the building was extremely tight. Once you took the width of circulation and staircase access away, the main living spaces were little more than three metres wide, consequently not an inch of space could be wasted. On the top floor, a roomy landing doubles as a study, while a laundry room has been created on the first floor to avoid having to carry washing downstairs to the basement. In the kitchen a neat office space screened by a sliding door is tucked between the units. Throughout the property storage packed with the paraphernalia of family living soars towards the ceiling, where crisp cornices have been carefully reinstated. It is a house where everything is in its place and there is a place for everything.

An equally striking aspect of the interior configuration is the inter-play between symmetry and asymmetry. Everywhere you look objects and finishes are echoed and reciprocated, adding to the cohesive feel of the whole. This spatial sophistication works clearly on the top floor where two bedrooms, separated by a sliding door, are almost mirror images of each other, with matching furniture visible through the transparent screening which is a feature of the confined environment. All the bathrooms gleam with the same calm-inducing mix of Moroccan mother-of-pearl tiles and textured Lavastone tiled floors from Copenhagen. Throughout there is a sense of transparency which establishes an orderliness in the lives of those who dwell there. Nowhere is this more apparent than as you step through the entrance door from the street. Rather than being enclosed by a narrow corridor, you are greeted by views into the main living space through a glass screen wall comprised of black Crittall full-height windows. This retains the required functional separation for means of escape purposes, yet also establishes the aesthetic openness as the main priority. One senses a typical moment of Stiff + Trevillion architect-client thought transfer, an echo of Dale Carnegie's theories on how to influence people: "Let the other fellow feel that the idea is his."[11]

Westbourne Grove Mews in the 1990s was a relatively down-at-heel place. By 2003 it had become fashionable, a west London Bond Street of high end brands. Too small and too fashionable with too many celebrity shoppers, it was time to move.

In 2003 they made the move to the northern edges of Notting Hill, to Acklam Road Studios within ear-shot of the Westway thundering above Portobello Green. It was a much less salubrious area but still recognisably Notting Hill and significantly more affordable. There weren't many celebrities around here. This was discernible when walking along the Golborne Road which ran into the northern end of Portobello. The street is a mix of ethnic eating experiences, low-grade 'antique' shops, tanning parlours, interior design shops and a few high street fashion houses, such as Ally Capellino. Moroccan mixes with French, Spanish and Portugese, with cafes such as Lisboa Patisserie, Cafe Oporto and buzzing Moroccan restaurants such as Le Marrakech, the Moroccan Experiance, a misspelling which can be forgotten when tasting the comforting snacks available at all times of the day and night. Further on there are Moroccan stalls selling seasoned Tajine and couscous, alfresco. Then, as you enter the northern end of Portobello Road, the casbah gives way to more archetypal London places like Cockney's Trad Pie 'N' Mash & Eels shop, Tattoo U and the Swanky Lash & Brow Bar. This is where marijuana is smoked openly in the street by third generation Rasta boys all in the shadow of a spanking new million pound apartment block. Called Orwell House, clearly irony is lost on the developer's PR company as its high spec luxury is all a million miles, and several million pounds away from Winston Smith and the perverse horrors of *1984*, George Orwell's landmark novel.

From the vibrant street scene with its spirit of understated creativity and quiet celebrity, to the quirky shops and diverse cultural influences provided by second and third generation immigrants, for Mike this was exactly what he wanted from his home territory, diametrically opposite to the stultifying home counties suburbia of his formative years. Full of aspiring people on the make who all believe they are on the way up. In a sense they are all right, in Portobello it is hard to fail. Although it is intimate and friendly, in a sense, big city mores prevail, importantly, people still keep their distance and are discreet, in these streets you can remain private if that is what you want.

When Stiff + Trevillion moved a few blocks away to the Woodfield Road studios in 2006, they soon discovered a suitable 'local' just around the corner. The Union Tavern was very down at heal in true *Withnail and I* style, which even for them, after all the years they had spent drinking at that archetypal 1950s boozer the Cock and Bottle off Westbourne Grove, this was too much. With its sticky floor finishes and cracked windows which gave drafty views over the canal, the establishment was in dire need of a makeover.

Never slow in proposing urban improvements to their locality, Stiff + Trevillion proposed a quick, low cost makeover. The brewery, jumped at the chance, and the leisure team knocked-out a basic scheme which was then handed to a local contractor, completing the project in one short weekend as a favour. Now Stiff + Trevillion 'owned' their own pub. The refurbishment was hardly up to the standard expected by their leisure clients, nevertheless it was enough. They had found their home.

Group photo of most of the
Stiff + Trevillion studio, 2013.

— The people you employ are your biggest asset and your biggest overhead.

— The cost of your offices will be a significant overhead, so ensure that it is giving you the space and image you need for the business. A good, but not extravagant office set up will impress clients and reward staff.

— Calculate your base cost, what you need to earn each month, and set up a management system that forecasts fees and cashflow. This will help to stabilise the practice finances.

— Agree to invoice fees on a monthly basis, it is better to get fees into the bank in small regular chunks. As well as covering monthly costs, alarm bells will ring much sooner this way.

— Take your responsibilities seriously and resource each job with a team that can be supported by the agreed fee.

— Have a practice policy on fees, talk to other practices and try to understand the market you are in. Adopt a minimum fee strategy, but be aware that this will need to flex in tougher economic times.

— Repeat work is the biggest sign of success, so treat each new job for an existing client with the same care and attention as the first.

— Identify and understand the markets you want to operate in and do not waiver. It is good to have an expertise in different specialisms and sectors.

— If successful projects are the vital organs of your business, then PR is the lifeblood. Carefully consider which awards and publications will be of most benefit. Peer group awareness and approval is as important as reaching out to potential clients.

— A marketing budget should be part of your base overhead costs, use it to refresh both printed and electronic media. Your website will often be the first port of call for a new client, update it and test it regularly.

— Look forward, plan for the future, bring in younger directors to provide fresh thinking and continuity.

CHAPTER 4 NOTES

1. Turn, Turn, Turn, with words adapted from The Bible, book of Ecclesiastes.

2. Czech Embassy, London, 1970, by Jan Bocan, Jan Sramek and Karel Stephansky, built in collaboration with Robert Matthew of Johnson-Marshall & Partners.

3. Shillam, Wendy, "Review of Latimer Place Studios" in *Architecture Today*, 141, p. 50.

4. Silver, Simon, "Space and Surface", in Stiff + Trevillion "black book".

5. Silver, "Space and Surface".

6. Part of a letter to Mike Stiff from Richard Reed, Co-CEO of innocent.

7. AAP (Architecture Appraisal Panel) for the Royal Borough of Kensington and Chelsea.

8. BREEAM stands for the Building Research Establishment Environmental Assessment Method.

9. Cool Britannia was a period of increased pride in the culture of the UK throughout the 1990s, inspired by 1960s pop culture.

10. Lutyens, Dominic, "Mayfly: Grand Designs Outdoors, A Natural Beauty", July 2013, p. 78.

11. Carnegie, Dale, *How to Win Friends and Influence People*, Random House, 2010.

Corner restaurant on the second floor of Selfridges department store, London, on the women's couture fashion floor. The style adopts an usually soft, feminine quality. Stiff + Trevillion worked closely with the Selfridges design team, their blended taste shows to good effect, 2013.

Conclusion

There is often genuine surprise when people find out that we started our business when we were so young. Were things easier then? Why did we do it rather than work for someone else?

There were few decent employment opportunities in the early 1980s, it was not an easy time for the construction industry, neither of us really wanted to build a career in a large commercial practice. The idea that self-employment gave you greater command of your time and destiny was persuasive, and the opportunity to work on a major international competition, albeit unpaid, was also attractive.

I have often wondered whether we set-up in business too soon after qualification, whether we would have learned more working for a good practice for a few years. We will never know, but it is fair to say that some of the most successful practices around today were spawned from Foster Associates and the Richard Rogers Partnership.

Starting from scratch means that every job, however small is of fundamental importance for two reasons. The fee income is essential and the practice needs to develop a body of work and demonstrate experience. The result is that early projects may well be fiddly, with difficult clients; the fees will be lower than they should be and the quality of the work variable as a result. The early ambition is to build, and a client is taking a risk with a young practice, as a result fees on a project are often reduced and more time is expended than can really be afforded. Most architects' early work will reflect this. It is not uncommon that this pattern becomes ingrained in the DNA of the

Under the Westway, painting by Mike Stiff, 2013. The Grand Union Canal near Stiff + Trevillion's office, with Trellick Tower in the distance.

business. Architects are naturally grateful to be given the opportunity to work on a juicy project, the fee is often secondary. In some ways fees are embarrassing to talk about, what we really want to convey to the client is a passion for architecture and in particular their project. It is quite astonishing, and probably unique to our profession, that architects commit themselves emotionally to the project. If there is a problem, the first question we ask ourselves is "what have we done wrong?"

It took us a long time to realise that we are first and foremost a business, as soon as you employ someone you have a responsibility and a duty to look after them. We have always held that once a fee is agreed we are morally obliged to do the work for that sum. Rarely have we gone back to seek additional fees, and if we have it is in circumstances where the brief has changed.

This may appear to be naïve to some readers, and I guess it is directly born out of the casual way the practice began, a loose association of like-minded friends, with the same ambitions, and no ego issues.

As the business grows the issues are just the same, it is a balance of resources (people), and workload (fees). Managing a practice is all about these two things, the bigger you become the more complex that relationship is and the more systems you need to manage it. Just consider the four key management tools of architectural business:

— Public Relations: getting the work.
— Human Resources: people are your asset.

— IT: the means of production.

— Financial control: looking after the money
once you had made it.

These four all carry a cost, and that cost will increase the larger the practice becomes. You can start a business with a sketchbook and a laptop, accounting can be managed with an in-and-out book and some envelopes. All of this changes the moment you employ someone, and this has become a much more complex thing to do in the 30 years since we started out.

When does an architectural practice get to a point where it cannot cope with these issues internally? There are certain stages in the development that are step changes, at these points a practice will need to employ an IT Manager, a full-time Financial Controller or an HR Director.

We believe that it is essential to maintain a balance between the flexibility and dynamism of a small start-up and an understanding of the business models that make for success. In our view the more an organisation becomes structured, the less efficient it is.

Always ask yourself why you took up architecture? Was it to design, think, draw or to be a Project Manager? Being an architect can be rewarding, it can be frustrating but it is never dull. We hope that our story communicates this idea, and it would be great to think that it may help some aspiring architects in the future.

Stiff + Trevillion

PHOTOGRAPHIC PERMISSIONS

p. 16   View of Western Avenue, section one roundabout. Courtesy English Heritage. Photo: Clive Boursnell.

p. 29   Maison de Verre. Courtesy Robert Vickery/Architectural Association Photo Library.

p. 35   View showing the demolition of the Euston Arch in the early 1960s. Courtesy English Heritage.

p. 38   Kimbell Art Museum, Fort Worth, Texas, constructed 1969–1972, north portico, Louis I Kahn, 1901–1974. Photo: Robert LaPrelle. Copyright Kimbell Art Museum, Fort Worth.

p. 50   Richards Medical Center. Courtesy University of Pennsylvania Archives.

p. 75   Sainsbury's Wing. Courtesy Valerie Bennett/Architectural Association Photo Library.

p. 98   Copyright www.bilderbuch-berlin. net/Kino International, Berlin 1968.

p. 122   Courtesy Art Institute of Chicago.

p. 162   Czech Embassy. Courtesy Architectural Press Archive/RIBA Library Photographs Collection.

ACKNOWLEDGEMENTS

Our particular thanks go to the current Stiff + Trevillion team: Selvei Al-Assadi, Ray Attfield, Stephen Ayles, Andrew Bell, Sam Blandy, Natalie Benes, Sean Crummey, Nick Delo, Chris Eaton, Lally Esguerra, Johnny Gordon, Emily Harris, James Hogan, Lee Hopwood, Joe Howland, Murad Imakaev, Tom Johnson, David Kahn, Celestria Kimmins, Yuki Kondo, Emily Lawley, Jazz Logue, Etsuko McGee, Magnus Menzefricke-Koitz, Ed Mullett, Nicole Tang, Hanneke van der Heijden, Davide De Giorgi, Jonathan Murray, Craig Watson, Armin Rose, Lance Routh, Rebecca Snow.

Stiff + Trevillion have worked with many excellent photographers over the years, but our thanks go to Kilian O'Sullivan whose photographs illustrate most of Chapter 4.

The following photographers' work is featured in this book:

Peter Cook (322 High Holborn), Peter Durant (Satsuma), Chris Gascoigne (Stüssy, Footpatrol, Copperfield Street), Dennis Gilbert (Hawkes House), Keith Hunter (Jamie's Italian, Aberdeen), Andrew Meredith (Selfridges), Kilian O'Sullivan (Costa, Pizza Express, RA, Café Anglais, Jamie's Italian, Pentonville Road, Designers Guild, Morley House, Portobello Dock, innocent, 1 Valentine Place, Heathview, Mayfly Cottage, Chepstow Villas, Phoenix Brewery, Team And Office Photography), Palladium Photodesign (Treptow Berlin), Paul Tyagi (Roke Manor Research), Morley von Sternberg (St Alban), Mathew Weinreb (wagamamma, City Rhodes), Alan Williams (Wateringbury, Egham)

Thanks to all at Artifice books on architecture for their patience and encouragement.

Finally, to Mark Dudek who wrote it.

Detail of the VIP lounge at the Sydney Contemporary 2013. The most recent in a series of Art Fairs designed by the practice for Tim Etchells.

INDEX

© 2014 Artifice books on architecture, the
architects and the authors. All rights reserved.

Artifice books on architecture
10A Acton Street
London
WC1X 9NG
t. +44 (0)207 713 5097
f. +44 (0)207 713 8682

sales@artificebooksonline.com
www.artificebooksonline.com

All opinions expressed within this publication
are those of the authors and not necessarily
of the publisher.

Designed by Amy Cooper-Wright at Artifice
books on architecture.

British Library Cataloguing-in-Publication
Data. A CIP record for this book is available
from the British Library.

ISBN 978 1 908967 33 6

No part of this publication may be
reproduced, stored in a retrieval system,
or transmitted, in any form or by any means,
electronic, mechanical, photocopying,
recording, or otherwise, without prior
permission of the publisher.

Every effort has been made to trace
the copyright holders, but if any have
been inadvertently overlooked the
necessary arrangements will be made
at the first opportunity.

Artifice books on architecture is an
environmentally responsible company.
Stiff + Trevillion: Practising Architecture
is printed on sustainably sourced paper.